PRACTICAL CRIMINOLOGY:
Cases and Materials

Second Edition

George Seibel

Morton College

A Prairie Avenue Press
Criminal Justice Classic

Practical Criminology: Cases and Materials
Second Edition
Copyright 2014 by George Seibel
ISBN 978-0-9829123-8-6

Library of Congress Catalog Card Number
2014 PEP 11214

Manufactured in the United States of America
By OneTouchPoint Ginnys, Austin, Texas

Word Processing by Judith Solomon

PRAIRIE AVENUE BOOKS
Box 217, Riverside, IL 60546

Publisher's Cataloging in Publication:

SEIBEL, George 1947-

Practical Criminology:
Cases and Materials
Second Edition

DEDICATION

To Nora and her Greatness

Other Books by George Seibel

TABLE OF CONTENTS

INTRODUCTORY COMMENTS

Over the past four decades or so I have often been very near to crime and criminal behavior. I began my career as a "street cop" on a tactical team on the South Side of Chicago. After a couple of years I became a Violent Crimes investigator and moved to the West Side. I then studied criminal justice and earned a couple of degrees, which entitled me to call myself a criminologist. Soon after, I found my way into the classroom as an instructor while continuing to work in the private sector as a cold case investigator.

Interestingly, my dual roles of having been trained both as a criminal investigator and criminologist were not nearly as compatible as one might think. The central focus of criminology is a body of theories as to why individuals commit crime. Virtually all of the theories are painfully limited in scope to the extent that even the uninitiated can readily identify a seeming fatal flaw in just about every notable theory. At the same time the theories in question seemed to have little in common with my own practical findings gathered while having dealt with hardcore members of the criminal community.

The inherent weaknesses in criminological theory not surprisingly resulted in a strain of the study called "critical criminology," which is really little more than one criminologist taking a lot of words to state the obvious as to why the theories of others are insufficient.

Clearly, my freshman-level students have readily engaged in the same pastime about one week into a new semester.

Instructor: The theory is that poverty breeds crime.
Student: But many poor people are honest and don't commit crimes.
Instructor: I know that.
Student: Then what's your point?

And so it was that the idea for *Practical Criminology: Cases and Materials* came to be. The result is that Part I identifies a large number of theories created over the past century or so. Each would then be tested based on what the author knows to be factual as to criminal behavior in Part II. Lastly, Part III would outline many of the specific ways in which criminal acts are taught, planned, carried out, and responded to by the police and courts. Just how much of criminology actually does have a practical application will be left to the individual reader to decide.

George Seibel
Morton College
July, 2009

FOREWORD TO SECOND EDITION

Five years ago the first edition of *Practical Criminology: Cases and Materials* was introduced. What made this work a stark contrast to other books on criminology was the attempt at making certain practical applications of what had been until that time, a largely theoretical subject.

The results were seemingly mixed. Most students were more easily able to grasp theories of criminology by having a practical application as a guide to understanding. By contrast, many criminologists were unimpressed by the effort to take the theory of apples and attempt to turn them into practical oranges. One thing many said had little or nothing to do with the other.

However, due to the academic support of a small group of colleagues, and my own sense of project viability, it was decided to dig deeper into the criminology hopper in search of more practical answers. Therefore, the second edition introduces an all new Part IV, discussing what researchers of delinquency and street gangs have found, and how such findings apply to what we are certain law enforcement knows about such issues.

The best ideas are often simple; therefore, the attempt of the second edition is to present new issues in the simplest manner possible. It is hoped that readers will enjoy a second journey into making practical sense of the theoretical world of criminology.

PART I

CRIMINOLOGY THEORIES

Criminologists have pondered reasons for crime and possible solutions for as long as there has been the written word. Today, criminology is based upon the accumulated findings of several centuries. That which follows is a brief overview of the mostly widely discussed theories.

Classical School

The Classical School of Criminology, which dates to the middle of the eighteenth century, is based on the accepted proposition that criminals choose to commit crimes after first weighing the consequences of their actions. According to the classical school individuals have free will to choose between either legal or illegal actions to get what they want. The theory takes the position that actors measure the potential pleasure derived from the act against the consequences of being caught and punished, thus classical theorists take the position that stiff punishment can deter crime.

The classical school was a reaction to an extremely unjust system of laws and punishments during the 1700s. Many laws were unwritten and applied without uniformity. For example, a child could be sent to prison for having disobeyed a parent. Punishment for many crimes included torture, mutilation, and beheading. And the more brutal the punishment, the more crime there was. Therefore by the mid-1700s social reformers began to take a more reasonable approach to punishment. One of them, Cesar Beccaria, introduced the first school of criminology which came to be known as the classical school.

In 1764 Beccaria presented a paper entitled, *On Crimes and Punishment*, which was a coherent plan for an enlightened justice system which would serve the people and not the monarchy. In the book Beccaria outlined the ways in which judges arbitrarily applied barbaric laws, and how essentially innocent alleged offenders were enslaved. Under new law, judges would be held to specific guidelines for administering punishment.

According to Beccaria the crime problem rested in, not bad people, but rather in bad laws. Henceforth, all persons would be treated equally before the law. Beccaria proposed the following guidelines for administering justice:

1) Laws should be used to maintain the social contract. Laws are the condition under which individuals, naturally independent, united themselves in society.
2) Only legislators should create laws. Lawmakers alone, not actors in the justice system, may create laws.
3) Judges should impose punishment only in accordance with the law. Strict guidelines for sentencing must be in place.

4) Judges should not interpret the law. Subjective views of the law are to be outlawed.
5) Punishment should be based on the pleasure/pain principle. Punishment should fit the degree of the act.
6) Punishment should be based on the act, not the actor. Status should play no role in the sentencing process.
7) Punishment should be prompt and effective. The quicker the punishment after the act, the more effective it will be (as to deterrence).
8) Capital punishment and torture should both be abolished.
9) It is better to prevent crimes than to punish them.

Beccaria's book had great influence on society and served as the basis for reform.

Notes on Classical School

The classical theory is based upon the proposition that individuals weight the advantages and disadvantages of embarking upon a criminal act. This concept then obviously can apply only to premeditated crimes. For the decision-making described by Beccaria, it might only occur during a period of time between the initial thought of committing the act and a subsequent decision either to act or not act. This position disregards spontaneous acts such as walking in on one's lover, seeing him/her with another, and an immediate response of raging violence. It is thus important to consider that a large percentage of everyday criminal acts are spontaneous and not premeditated in nature.

Positivist Criminology

Biological Determination

In 1859 Charles Darwin published *Origin of Species* in which he refuted biblical notions of creation, but rather stated that evolution came about through adaptive mutation and natural selection. The theory was based upon survival of the fittest in the struggle for existence. Then in 1871 Darwin publicly traced man to the apes. Darwin thereafter moved researchers toward biological answers to crime and general human behavior. Old ideas that demons and animal spirits could explain human behavior were replaced by new scientific principles as the social sciences came into being. The combined forces of positivism and evolution moved the field of criminology from a philosophical to a scientific perspective.

Early Ideas About Criminal Traits

Early on a variety of physical characteristics and disfigurements were said to characterize "bad and evil" in individuals. Throughout the ages people with long hair and physical deformities were viewed as having a great potential for acting out violence and other crimes. Indeed, in the Middle Ages it was thought that when more than one individual was suspected of a crime, the least attractive of the lot was almost certainly the guilty party. During that time period it was widely accepted that criminals were born and not made.

Cesare Lombroso (1835-1909) replaced the concept of free will as the principle that dictated criminal behavior with that of determinism, seeking his answers through research and scientific experimentation. His theory of the born criminal was based upon the theory that criminals are a lower form of life, less developed than other persons and closer to ape-like ancestors. He argued that criminals often have huge jaws and oversized canine teeth, which are used to tear apart and eat raw meat. He also stated that the arm span of criminals is often greater than their height, the same as in apes who use their forearms when walking along the ground.

Lombroso used the term "atavistic stigmata" to describe the physical features of a creature at an earlier level of development prior to becoming fully human. He stated that an individual who is born with any five stigmata is indeed a born criminal. About one-third of all criminals at that time met those standards.

Lombroso also discussed differences between male and female criminals. "It is the prostitute," he said, "who represents the born criminal among women. They have a childlike moral sense and are prone toward vengeance and refined violence."

In addition to the born criminal, Lombroso also categorized the insane criminal, who are not born criminals, and criminaloids. Insane criminals become that way due to a change in their brains which does not allow them to understand right from wrong. Criminaloids are a vaguely described group who are made up of habitual criminals and those who commit crimes of passion.

Somatotype School of Criminology

This school of criminology relates body build to behavior. This theory became popular during the first half of the twentieth century. It originated with the work of Ernest Kretchmer (1888-1964), who pointed to three distinct body types: the asthenic, slightly built, not well-muscled, with narrow shoulders; the athletic build, muscular and strong, usually above average height; and finally the pyknic frame, medium height, rounded body, massive neck and broad face. Kretchmer then related these body types to various psychic disorders — pyknics to manic depression, athletics and asthenics to schizophrenia, and so on.

William Sheldon (1898-1967) utilized Kretchmer's work in developing his own group of body types: the endomorph, the mesomorph, and the ectomorph. Sheldon claimed that endomorphs, those strong, muscular, and athletic types, were most likely to be involved in criminal behavior.

Psychological Determinism

At the start of the twentieth century psychologists used their new techniques of measurement to the study of measurement.

Administering intelligence tests to inmates in asylums, jails, and prisons were particularly popular. Through this testing researchers were interested in weighing the relationship between mental deficiencies and crime. In 1914 Henry Goddard (1868-1957) examined certain intelligence tests that had been given to inmates and concluded that 25 to 50 percent of the people in prison had intellectual defects that made them incapable of managing their own affairs. These ideas were accepted until World War I when it was determined that the intelligence testing scores of draftees were lower than that of the inmates. As a result of that study and others like it, intelligence quotient measures largely disappeared as a basis for explaining criminal behavior.

Sociological Determinism

Andre' Michel Guerry (1802-1866) was one of the first scholars to disagree with the free-will doctrine of classical criminology. Guerry studied the relation of crime data to such factors as poverty, sex, and age, concluding that society, and not free will was responsible for criminal behavior. He found that wealthy regions of France had the highest rate of crimes against property, but very low crimes against persons rates. Thus he concluded that wealthy individuals were highly sought after victims who attracted criminal attention. As such, criminals went to where wealth was to commit crimes.

Emile Durkheim

A major approach as to social factors of crime causation asks how crime occurs in the first place, and also how it is related to the functioning of a society. Emile Durkheim (1858-1917) was at the center of such research.

Durkheim is recognized as one of the founders of sociology. He stated that crime is a perfectly normal function of society. He contended that crime should disappear from society only when all members of society had the same values, and that such a goal for all individuals to want the same things is neither possible nor desirable. He went so far as to say that in certain circumstances crime is necessary if society is to advance.

Durkheim stated that all societies have both crime and sanctions. In strong cohesive societies laws are enforced to maintain the group solidarity. By contrast, in a large heterogeneous society laws are enforced and criminals punished in the interest of protecting the victim.

Psychology and Criminality
Psychoanalytic Theory

The psychoanalytic theory of criminology attributes delinquency and criminal behavior to an issue of conscience which may be
1) So overbearing that it arouses feelings of guilt, or
2) So weak that it cannot control the individual's impulses, or

3) So weak that it cannot control a need for immediate gratification.

The above concept stems from Sigmund Freud (1856-1939), the father of psycho-analysis, who suggested that criminal behavior may result from an overactive conscience that results in excessive guilt feelings. Freud noted that such individuals commit crimes in hope of being apprehended and punished for their acts.

Freud used the terms superego, ego, and id in explaining issues dealing with the conscience. The conscience or superego might be so weak or defective that impulses become out of control. In such instances the ego, which acts to control impulses and inhibitions is rendered useless. Thus the id, which encourages seeking pleasure and satisfaction, may run out of control.

When one has an insufficiently developed superego, criminals are likely to act out without regard for negative consequences, a condition which adequately explains the type of out-of-control behavior seen in certain youths as well as adult serial offenders.

Moral Principles and Social Norms

Basic moral principles and social norms are learned through social interaction and role playing. Children learn how to be moral by reasoning with others who are at a higher level of moral development. Research by Lawrence Kohlberg involved placing individuals with low moral reasoning in the company of persons with significantly higher moral reasoning. The results were generally that positive influences from the experience increased their level of moral reasoning.

Social Learning Theory
     This theory of criminology maintains that criminal and delinquent behavior is learned through the same psychological processes as all non-delinquent behavior. Behavior is learned when it is reinforced or rewarded and not learned when it is not reinforced. Behavioral modeling occurs when children learn how to act by mimicking the acts of others. Chances of negative modeling occur most often when the learning occurs in communities where crime is most common. Negative modeling is also highly active when children are placed geographically near older members of the criminal community.

Differential Association
     This theory is based upon the highly simplistic proposition that all children come in contact with both honest individuals and those who commit criminal and delinquent acts. If the sum of the interactions is greater with honest people, the subjected child will be honest. But when the majority of interactions are with criminals, the result will be the creation of another criminal.

     It is to be noted that differential association, as a strict social theory, has a total disregard for individual differences in the subject. The issue of right from wrong does not come into play, nor does it make a difference whether or not the subject was loved and nurtured in the home.

Personality

Investigators have looked at the personality traits of the criminal versus the non-criminal. Much of this work has taken place within jails and prisons where researchers determined that inmates are more immature, impulsive, hostile, and self-centered than non-criminals.

Criminologists also attempt to predict behavior when inmates are confronted with prison discipline. Also of interest is whether the inmates will take steps to stay free after release from incarceration. Research results clearly disclose that personality traits are not accurate predictors of criminal behavior, either inside or outside of prison.

Researchers have attempted to determine the extent to which normal personality traits operate in criminals. Indications are that mainstream inmates are more pleasant and social than those inmates isolated from the general population.

Finally, researchers have looked into personality differences between violent offenders as opposed to those who commit property crimes. Similarly, comparisons have been made between first-time offenders and life-long criminals. In general, the personality traits of the relative groups were not significantly different from one another.

Mental Disorders and Crime

It is difficult for psychiatrists to derive data that would help decide which criminals are mentally ill. The medical profession typically views mental illness as an absolute condition — one is either a psychotic or one is not a psychotic.

Psychopathy is a term which is defined as an anti-social personality. This personality is notable for an inability to learn from one's negative experiences. Other traits of psychopathy include a lack of warmth and most importantly, no sense of guilt. Observers state that the psychopath wears a mask so that he/she appears to be well adjusted. However, in the course of time it becomes apparent that the psychopath feels no sense of shame, is insincere, and is likely to engage in both verbal and physical abuse without provocation.

Genetics and Criminality
The XYY Syndrome

Chromosomes are the basic structures that contain genes, the biological material that makes individuals unique. Each person has twenty-three pairs of inherited chromosomes. Gender, skin complexion, hair and eye colors are all determined in this manner. A male gets an X chromosome from his mother and a Y chromosome from the father, while a female receives an X chromosome from both the mother and father. There are occasions where a defect in production of egg or sperm results in genetic abnormalities, one of which is the XYY chromosomal male. The XYY male receives two Y chromosomes from the father. About 1 in 1000 males have this genetic composition. One study of inmates in maximum-security state hospitals disclosed that the frequency of XYY males was twenty times greater than among the general population. XYY males tend to be tall, violent, and aggressive. They are also specifically prone to sexual violence.

Twin Studies

In an effort to determine whether or not crime is genetically predetermined, researchers have compared identical and fraternal twins. Identical twins develop from a single fertilized egg that divides into two embryos. These twins share all of their genes. Fraternal twins develop from two separate eggs, both fertilized at the same time. They share about one-half of their genes.

Since the prenatal and postnatal family environments are basically the same, greater behavioral similarity between identical twins than between fraternal twins would support an argument for genetic predisposition.

In the 1920s a German physician, Johannes Lange, found thirty pairs of same-sex twins — thirteen identical and seventeen fraternal pairs. One of each pair was a known criminal. Lange found that in ten of the thirteen pairs of identical twins, both were criminals. In only two of seventeen pairs of fraternal twins, both were criminals. This limited range research strongly indicated that there was in fact a strong genetic predisposition toward crime.

Adoption Studies

One way to separate the influence of inherited traits from that of environmental conditions is to study infants separated at birth from their natural parents and randomly adopted or placed in foster homes. It was then possible to determine whether the adopted child's behavior more closely mirrored that of the natural parents or of the adopted parents.

The largest adoptive study took place in Denmark where over 14,000 adoptions were followed. Data was collected in four ways: subjects who had natural and adoptive parents where neither were criminals, where subjects had both natural and adoptive parents who were criminals, where only the natural parent was criminal, and where only the adoptive parent was criminal.

In the first category where neither parent was criminal, 13.5 percent of the subjects were criminal. Where both natural and adoptive parents were criminals, 24.5 percent of the boys also were criminals. Where only the adoptive parent was criminal, 14.7 of the boys were convicted of crimes, and where only the natural parent was criminal, 20 percent of the boys were convicted of offenses. These findings support the claim that the criminality of the natural parents has more influence on the child than that of the adoptive parents. Thus, in this instance at least one might conclude that biological issues are of greater influence upon crime determination than are environmental issues.

Labeling Theory

Basic Assumptions of the Labeling Theory

During the 1940s a sociologist named Edward Lemert created certain basic assumptions as to labeling. He stated that many individuals act in ways in which they might be identified as a delinquent, however only a few individuals ever are labeled thusly. The reason for this disparity rests in the fact that there are two categories of deviant acts, primary and secondary.

Primary deviations are those acts which bring on the initial social response. Such acts do not affect the individual's self-concept. It is the secondary deviations, the acts that follow society's initial response to the primary deviation, that are the main concern. These are the acts which result from the change in self-concept brought about by the labeling process. The path to crime as seen by Lemert follows:

1) An individual commits a simple primary deviation such as throwing a stone at a neighbor's car.

2) There is an informal social reaction; the neighbor gets angry.

3) The individual continues to break rules—other primary deviations—and lets the neighbor's dog out of the yard.

4) There is increased but still primary social reaction. The neighbor tells the parents of the individual.

5) The individual commits a more serious primary deviation and is caught shoplifting at the drug store.

6) There is a formal reaction; the youth is adjudicated as being "delinquent" in juvenile court.

7) The youth is now labeled "delinquent" by the court and "trouble" by neighbors, peers, and others.

8) The youth now sees himself/herself as a delinquent and joins other troubled youths.

9) The individual commits a far more serious secondary deviant act by robbing the gas station with his/her new troubled friends.

10) The individual returns to juvenile court to face more offenses and takes on a completely deviant lifestyle.

According to Lemert secondary deviance sets in after the community has become aware of primary deviance. The theory states that it is a form of injustice the youth faces when his/her company is no longer sought by mainstream law-abiding individuals. At the same time Lemert states that employment opportunities shrink, and police begin to watch the individual. Thus the individual's avenues into mainstream society are taken from him/her by the stigma of the court having designated the youth as being delinquent.

Labeling Experiment

Empirical investigations of labeling theory have been carried out by researchers in many disciplines. A group of researchers arranged to have eight sane volunteers apply for admission to mental hospitals. Each of the eight complained of hearing voices, a primary symptom of schizophrenia. However, immediately upon having been admitted the fake patients behaved normally. The experiences of the patients illustrated the problems facing those having been labeled. Medical staffs treated the fake patients as schizophrenics. They interpreted normal behavior of the fake patients as manifestations of illness. An early arrival at the breakfast table was seen as exhibiting "oral aggressive" behavior. A patient seen writing was referred to as being a "compulsive note-taker." When the patients were finally discharged, they were labeled as being "schizophrenics in remission." It is interesting to note that though the medical staff was convinced that the fake patients were mentally ill, the same was not true of the patients who commonly assumed that the fake patients were journalists.

These findings support criminological labeling theory. Once the sane individuals were labeled as being mentally ill, they were unable to remove the label by acting normally. Even after they had seemingly recovered and were released they were still labeled "schizophrenic in remission," which implied that future episodes were to be expected.

The Anomie Theory of Emile Durkheim

One perspective of society is accomplished by looking at its component parts in an effort to see how they relate to one another. One views the structure of society to see how it functions. In a stable society where its parts operate smoothly, the social arrangements are functional. Such societies are marked by consensus, cohesion, and cooperation. But when the component parts are arranged in such a manner that they threaten the social order, they are dysfunctional. For example, within a class-oriented society the classes tend to be in conflict. One tiny building block taken from the foundation can send the entire structure tumbling. The functions of all the parts are at the mercy of one another.

Durkheim was primarily interested in the effects of social change and believed that when a simple society becomes more complex, the intimacy needed to sustain a common set of norms declines. Groups become fragmented and the goals and objectives of each new part vary from one another. With the absence of a common set of rules, the actions and wishes of one segment of society may clash with those of another. As behaviors and actions become unpredictable, the system eventually breaks down, and the society is in a state of anomie.

Durkheim presented much of his work on anomie within a discussion of suicide. He claimed that anomic suicides are greatest in times of sudden economic change, whether the change was unexpected prosperity or economic depression. In times of intense sudden change people are abruptly thrown into an unfamiliar way of life. Rules which once guided behavior no longer apply.

As to criminological applications of anomie, Durkheim believed that human desires are boundless. Society then places social rules which place a realistic limit on aspirations and goals. These limitations are internalized within an individual and thus make it possible to feel fulfilled and satisfied with that which one has. But with a sudden burst of prosperity, people's expectations change. When old sanctions no longer determine how rewards are gained among members of society, there is no longer any restraint on what people want. Then the system breaks down. Thus, whether sudden change causes great prosperity or economic hardship, the result is the same — anomie.

Strain Theory

Robert Merton developed the strain theory based in response to anomie. He stated that the actual problem was not caused by sudden change, but rather by a social structure which presents the same goals to all of its members without giving them equal opportunity of gaining them. Merton stated that societies promote desirable symbols of success but the social structure fails to offer all members of the society an equal means of obtaining them. Once society blocks legitimate opportunities for gaining the sought-after item to sizable portions of the population, the result is anti-social behavior taking place in pursuit of that goal.

Cultural Deviance Theories

The cultural deviance theory attributes crime to a set of values peculiar to the lower class. Adherence to the lower-class value system, which determines behaviors in inner-city areas, causes conflict with society's laws. Both strain and cultural deviance locate the causes of crime within the poorest communities, where individuals are more likely to follow their own system of values as opposed to written laws.

Thus, cultural deviance theorists view crime as resulting from cultural values that often demand behavior in violation of the law. The three primary cultural deviance theories are social disorganization, differential association, and cultural conflict.

Social disorganization theory focuses on the development of high-crime areas associated with the disintegration of conventional values caused by urbanization and other social issues. As stated in other sections of this work, social disorganization is notable for residents' general inability to perform routine life-skill functions.

Differential association theory, which is covered extensively elsewhere within, states that people learn to commit crimes due to associations with others who commit crimes and have anti-social attitudes and values. When most interactions are with honest individuals, the person too will be honest.

Cultural conflict theory states that different groups and classes within society learn different conduct norms—rules governing conduct—and that the accepted norms of some groups may clash with conventional middle-class values. All three theories contend that criminals and delinquents do conform—but to those norms that deviate from those of the dominant middle class.

PART II

POLICE AND CRIMINALS

ARTICLE 1 — *Policing Within*
a Conflict Society

Conflict Theory Revisited

Conflict theory advocates take the position that there are varying segments of society which do not hold the same values, goals, and aspirations as do middle-class groups. While most individuals follow a path toward long-term gratification—go to school, become a professional, buy a home, get married, and have a family—other groups of people reject that lifestyle. Those in conflict with those values are concerned with short-term gratification based upon monetary gain by either legal or illegal means. Since such individuals are in conflict with middle-class society, they generally see the police as the enemy, as a tool of the powerful to keep them essentially powerless. Such perspectives are often found in poor inner-city communities. Alcohol and street drug use are often a part of the conflict lifestyle, as moving into an altered state is a form of instant gratification.

A View of a Conflict-Based Community

Success is measured in conflicted areas by one's willingness and ability to carry out the most daring crimes. Just as children in middle-class communities are awarded trophies, ribbons, and plaques for academic, athletic, and performing arts achievements, members of conflicted society, too, have their own awards.

It is not unusual for the police to enter the home of a criminal offender only to see Polaroid photos framed and sitting atop a coffee table depicting a gang of robbers sitting alongside a table covered with money, guns, ski masks, and duct tape used in a successful crime. Certainly, such trophies establish the extent of the conflict which exists between middle-class society and the criminal subculture.

The open manner in which criminal acts are celebrated also acts to pass along their "crime is normal" attitude from one generation to the next. Such rejection of middle-class values is often demonstrated by street gang members who photograph small children flashing gang signs while wearing gang attire and colors.

The celebration of illegal activities among youthful individuals serves to reinforce criminal behaviors and further reject middle-class values from one generation to the next.

Self-Developed Criminal Reputations

Status within the criminal community turns certain individuals into living legends. Four members of one major city street gang were well known to be killers of many. All went to prison, then each was paroled back to the streets at about the same time. The quartet teamed up to form a home invasion gang. Each Thursday night when the large

34

"dope bags" were in stock for the upcoming weekend, they would rob anywhere between 10 and 15 dope dealers of their drugs and money.

In general terms the robbed drug dealers had limited choices. They could take on known killers and hope to survive, call the police and report their drugs having been taken, or they might simply chalk up their business loss. After having lost tens of thousands of dollars in street drugs, one long-time dealer did contact a police detective he trusted and reported the multiple crimes. The detectives then went about rounding up the killers, but not before one of the bandits jumped from an eighth-floor window, landed feet first on a blacktop lot, and made his way several blocks before being apprehended. Thus, one criminal reputation was enhanced to the extent that he came to be known as "Soul Superman" for his survival abilities.

———————

Criminal reputations are fostered by the open nature of talk among members of conflict society members. The general belief is that everyone on the street corner loathes the police enough so that bragging and otherwise recounting criminal offenses is a totally safe practice.

Members of the criminal community speak freely among themselves regarding their illegal activities due to a belief that the police are uniformly disliked within the criminal subculture. Such discussions are mandatory to the extent that offenders get their due acclaim, as one cannot gain credit for having committed an offense unless he/she admits to it.

However, bright and open-minded police investigators are able to penetrate the criminal code of silence through the development of confidential informants. To the extent that evidence may be gathered in this manner clearly states that the level of conflict between certain members of the criminal subculture and certain members of the police is clearly overstated.

A survey of the everyday behaviors of members of the criminal subculture discloses that in addition to committing violations of the law, many individuals behave in generally offensive ways.

Case Study

A prostitute's date was shot and killed in an inner-city alley before dawn. While the man engaged with the woman, her pimp approached and announced a robbery. When the victim attempted pulling away in his car, the gunman shot and killed him. The next evening the case was the lead story on the evening television news. The killer entertained a group of ten members of the criminal community on a street corner by bragging all about his exploits. The killer believed that his boasting about having committed the murder was safe talk. However, what he overlooked was that one of the men being told about the crime had a cousin who had been abused by the killer many years before. Thus, when he knew a police investigator he thought he could trust, it was a simple matter of confiding in him about the identity of the offender.

There are countless variations of the case study in the sense that many members of the criminal community violate others on an ongoing basis. Many criminals are bullies; others commit offenses while under the influence of alcohol or drugs so that they may not actually recall whom they have victimized in the past. Such individuals "hustle" others, taking advantage of others at every turn. For all of these reasons, many members of the criminal community are willing to tell what they know in that their general dislike toward the police is not as great as their dislike for the criminal doing the bragging.

Differential Association Revisited

A theory of criminology based on the principle that an individual becomes delinquent because of an excess of definitions learned that are favorable to violation of law over definitions learned that are unfavorable to violation of law.

Case Study

The crime was rare in the sense that there had been both a burglary and armed robbery associated with the offense. The owner of an inner-city currency exchange entered his business early on a Saturday morning to open for the day. As he entered the vault area a masked individual confronted him with a pistol and ordered him to open the safe. It was then that the victim first noticed that the gunman had apparently tunneled a hole through the wall connected to a vacant store. The victim turned over some $15,000 to the offender who then fled on foot.

When police investigators arrived they asked the victim to describe the gunman. When told that the offender was four feet tall, the police assumed that the victim meant something else but that is exactly how tall he said the gunman had been. There also had been another bit of evidence connected to the case. The victim was certain that a wooden toothpick was sticking out of the offender's mouth and through the ski mask he wore.

The police investigation centered on searching for extremely short robbers to no avail for a week or two. Then the investigators had occasion to be in an area several miles from the robbery when they saw a youth of perhaps ten years of age dressed like an adult gangster standing with a group of adults on a street corner. The youth had a cigarette in one corner of his mouth, a toothpick on the other, and had just finished taking a drink from a community bottle of wine being passed around. The investigators called the little suspect over to the car and asked his name, which he said was Robin Hood. When asked his real name, he replied that Robin Hood is all he had ever been called for as long as he could remember.

During the ride to the investigative headquarters Robin Hood explained that he was ten years old, that his mother had died when he was a baby, and that he had been brought up by a series of "street people, mostly junkies, pimps, and whores." He slept at various crack houses and ate whatever the street people happened to be eating on street corners.

Youth officers in the area were notified and had not had interactions with the youth, so they called the area where the child had been picked up. The out-of-area youth officers knew Robin Hood well, stating that he had been picked up for numerous robberies since he was age six. He had been made a ward of the state, and variously sent to first foster homes, then state run group homes; however he never stayed more than a day anywhere before fleeing back to his life on the streets. As far as anyone could tell, Robin Hood was probably telling the truth when he said that he was unable to identify a single letter of the alphabet and had never been inside a school.

The police investigators and the youth officers then questioned him about the currency exchange crime.

Police: What do you know about a tunnel job into a currency exchange on Damen Avenue?

Robin: You askin' me because I'm the only dude on the street who could fit through that hole.

Police: How did you get inside?

Robin: The only reason I'll talk to you is because I'm ten. Got to be twelve to be charged with a crime. (He was correct as to the law in that state.)

Police: How do you know about the law?

Robin: Went to a place where they were building a house and stole a sledgehammer and a pickaxe. After dark I used the hammer to knock the padlock off the door of the abandoned store. Then I picked a hole in the wall until it was big enough for me to crawl through to get into the money room.

Police: Then you waited for the man to open up?

Robin: Took a hit of speed (a stimulant drug) to stay awake.

Police: Then you put the gun on the man and took the money?

Robin: And he gave me $17,000.

Police: How did you get back to your hood?

Robin: Taxi. Gave him a hundred big ones for a tip.

Police: Who helped you with all of this?

Robin: Did this all alone because I learned all this all my life. One dude steals from building places (construction sites), and so that's where I got the idea about rippin' off the tools. I know a chump who just got paroled who specializes in tunnel burglaries so I listened to him talk about how he does it. And then the gun part is easy because robbery is my usual thing.

Police:	Where's the money?
Robin:	Threw a party, did some drugs, had some ladies . . .

Analysis

Robin Hood had spent all ten years of his life at the center of drug use, prostitution, and violence. He had no parents, no church or school, and no other socializing influences which might have made him reluctant to commit acts which are violations of the law. Since those who periodically raised him were themselves members of the criminal element, whatever illegal acts he committed were unlikely to have been met with negative consequences.

The child had learned, as Sutherland suggests, the specific manner to commit a variety of crimes required to carry out his plot, which led to his seizing a large amount of money. It is also significant that the money was spent on instant gratification desires, a predictable condition within lower-class society. Perhaps the most remarkable aspect of this case study, apart from the youth's tender age, was his knowledge of juvenile justice law, which in this case prohibited his being charged with any criminal act at his age of ten. This was from a child who had never been in a formal school setting.

Crime is Normal Revisited

Within certain communities—usually in lower-class society—crime is considered to be a normal function of everyday life. The social stigma often attached to committing criminal offenses is simply not present.

Case Study

Tactical officers had made an unusually large number of burglary arrests over a matter of only several weeks' time. Then just past midnight they responded to a call of a silent alarm at a warehouse. As their squad car pulled up to the warehouse entrance, a fellow ran from within the building and surrendered. The officers, used to interior searches and foot chases connected to commercial burglaries, could not quite figure out why the burglar seemed so willing to give himself up.

Once at the police station the arrestee asked what would happen to him if he were to plead guilty in court the next morning. The officers told him that based on his having no prior felony convictions, he would probably be given probation. The officers then became even more confused when their arrestee seemed disappointed at the prospect of probation.

Finally, one of the officers asked the arrestee just what it was that was going on. It was then that the burglar came clean. It seems that word had spread throughout the criminal community that the state prison system had recently started an electronics education program for inmates. The result was that petty burglars were lining up to get arrested so that they might attend prison, learn electronics, and be released as master burglars capable of defeating any alarm system anywhere.

Analysis

One might first wonder what prison officials might have been thinking by offering electronics courses to individuals whose work is based on making successful illegal entries into buildings. However, beyond the scope of penal administration is the amazing proposition that members of the criminal subculture would actually try to be arrested, tried, convicted, and incarcerated all in the interest of learning skills to be a better burglar.

In order for this condition to come about it was first required that members of the criminal community learned of the availability of the electronics courses. Secondly, the information had to be discussed as being significant and passed along from one potentially interested party to the next. Lastly, and most significantly, those who took part in the plan uniformly saw no social stigma attached to being labeled a felony inmate, nor must they have been concerned with what was actually involved in terms of having to serve prison time.

IQ and Delinquency Revisited

Hirschi and Hindelang concluded that IQ is an even more important factor in predicting crime than is either race or social class. They found significant differences in IQ among criminal and non-criminal populations within like racial and social groups.

Case Problem

Huey, a fifteen-year-old member of a major city street gang, has been tested as having the IQ of a six-year-old child. He is neither mean nor violent and is allowed to be a part of the street gang due to his ability to provide members with comic moments, and his willingness to run errands.

On a given night Huey has joined other gang members in drinking wine and smoking pot. Gang members then begin in a game of telling Huey to do more and more outrageous acts, such as knock over a large garbage can, then knocking out the lens on a stop-and-go light. He does each and then poses for applause from the gang members.

A gang member then tells him to pull the driver out of the next car that stops at the light on the corner where they congregate, then to drive away with the car. Gang members yell back and forth making bets as to whether or not Huey will continue to follow their instructions.

A car then pulls up to the light, which is being driven by an elderly woman. Huey rips open the driver's side door and yanks the tiny, frail lady from within the car like a ragdoll. Huey jumps into the car and slams it into gear and floors the gas pedal, running over the victim's neck in the process.

———————————

Huey is charged with murder and five of the gang members who instructed him as to what to do are charged with solicitation to commit murder. All are convicted in adult criminal court.

The question raised is whether Huey had the capacity to understand the difference between knocking over a garbage can and the carjacking which ended up taking a life. Had he not been severely low functioning, the act likely would not have happened. By contrast, there can be little debate as to the criminal responsibility of the gang members who manipulated Huey into performing the act.

ARTICLE 6 — IQ and Criminal Decision Making

Case Problem

A suburban construction worker had been visiting his mother in the inner city. Before starting the trip home he stopped at a package goods liquor store. He left his car running at the curb as he entered the store. As he exited the store he was hit over the head with a large piece of wood and rendered unconscious.

Three brothers then rode around with the victim in his own car planning what to do next. They found a handgun inside the car, then argued extensively over which of the offenders had the right to shoot the victim first. They then drove to a vacant lot where the gun was test-fired into an abandoned car, and it was found to be in good working order. The offenders then pried open the trunk lid of the abandoned car before each shot the victim once in the head. They then tossed the victim inside the trunk leaving him for dead.

The next morning patrol officers located the victim's car being driven nearby the initial crime scene. The driver was then turned over to investigators for interrogation, which follows.

| Police: | Why were you driving the victim's car knowing that we'd be looking for you? |
| Suspect: | It still had gas in it. |

Analysis

The suspect's response to the police implies that he was actually unable to associate having been caught for a major crime with the fact that he continued driving the car twelve hours after it had been reported taken in the shooting. Though it is speculative as to whether the case would have been solved had the suspect ditched the car, what is certain is that he was arrested when he was as a direct result of having kept possession of the car.

A second issue dealing with intelligence level surfaces as to the manner in which the suspect told of his argument with his brothers over the opportunity to shoot the victim before the others. His matter-of-fact manner with the police would indicate that the suspect thought that such disagreements are a normal function of everyday life.

ARTICLE 7 — Is It a Crime to Hate the Police?

Crime is Normal Revisited

When children from middle-class communities are late coming home from school, parents assume that the soccer game went to overtime. When inner-city children are late, parents fear for good reason that they may have fallen victim to a stray bullet or a random attack. Violence, bloodshed, and guns on the street are a normal function of inner-city life. Is it then any wonder that crime also becomes an accepted aspect of some communities?

Laws are seen as laws of the powerful and its agents as evil tools of repression. So many residents of such communities simply refuse to become participants in the criminal justice system. When witnesses to crimes, they turn their heads. When victims, they retaliate in kind rather than to involve the authorities.

Case Study — Remorse and Juvenile Justice

Police on patrol respond to a call of shots fired on the street. They quickly note that a skinny kid is running from the area of the loud reports. The police pursue and recover a loaded pistol which was recently fired. The arrestee is taken to the station and juvenile officers respond to process him.

The juvenile officers learn that the arrest is the first for the fourteen-year-old, so under most circumstances the child would receive a station adjustment, be turned over to a parent, and be diverted from juvenile court. However, when asked where he got the gun, the child refuses to talk. His refusal to divulge where he got the gun is taken as a sign of lack of remorse for his act, so he is sent to court.

Such discretion as to adjudication choices is common for youth officers. However, in this case is the youthful offender being sent to court for carrying a firearm or for scoffing in the face of a police authority he has been brought up not to believe in? The second question thus becomes one of whether the youth is a greater threat to society based upon a choice not to participate in what he feels is not relevant to him, than had he demonstrated sorrow for his act.

The argument might be made that the decision not to talk to the police actually is the act for which the youth was sent to court, and that what may be construed as defiance on the part of the youth should not be taken as a valid indication of his being of greater danger to society than a second youth who agreed to cooperate with the police.

Lower-Class Values Revisited

It is commonly accepted that among the traits valued by lower-class youths are toughness and excitement.

Police Placement Within the Organization

Police officers are able to control and model their work assignments and duties in several ways. Those seeking action and ongoing interactions with dangerous individuals are likely to make initial application to major city departments with significant inner-city areas noted for high crime rates. Similarly, action-oriented officers may seek specialized assignments connected to crime-fighting activities such as tactical units and criminal investigation. Personnel assigned to such positions are commonly referred to as "street cops."

By contrast, officers who are fearful of being placed in dangerous situation, or those who simply wish for a more quiet work environment, are able to apply to quiet rural or suburban departments. Additionally, officers employed in major city departments earmarked by high crime rates also have ways in which to avoid danger. They may accomplish such a goal by seeking inside positions such as front desk officer, lock-up keeper, or an assignment in the police administration offices. In other situations officers not wishing to be near danger might become traffic enforcement specialists or ask transfer to less dangerous police districts.

Criminal Place Within the Subculture

When violent offenders speak freely about their reasons for committing crimes, many indicate that in addition to whatever monetary gain may be involved, they do it for the "rush." Thus it becomes clear that many members of the criminal community are excitement seekers. To the extent that offenders seek excitement, that makes them similar to police officers who seek dangerous police assignments.

Criminologists have long stated that criminal status is accorded offenders in the same manner that education and athletic prowess is acknowledged within other segments of society. However, it is also important to note that not all offenders hold equal status. Street-corner society is configured according to varying amounts of status based upon the nature of the crimes committed. The more dangerous and daring the crime, the greater the status granted. Thus armed robbers, home invaders, and other "shooters" gather together on certain street corners where shoplifters and sneak thieves would not be welcome. Those less daring offenders would gather together in their own place in a much less conspicuous place.

Police-Criminal Comparisons

Armed robbery is a dangerous crime, not only for the victims but for offenders as well.

A robber must be concerned with a pair of negative possibilities — that they may attempt to rob an individual who might also be armed and eager to resist the robbery attempt. The other fear is that police might observe the crime as it occurs and respond with gunfire. Clearly then, armed robbery is a dangerous crime to commit. The offender must immediately gain control of the victim and gain his/her cooperation so that the offense occurs without complications. Similarly, the offender must also be willing to use his/her firearm against a victim intent upon resisting the crime.

Compare the way in which a "street cop" correctly responds to a police call of "robbery in progress." He/She responds quickly to the crime scene, takes control of the situation by drawing his/her own firearm upon the offender, and announcing his/her office.

Clearly, the manner in which violent offenders successfully rob and the way in which "street cops" respond to such robberies call for precisely the same set of dynamics, based upon fearlessness, a willingness to confront danger, the ability to take control by use of orders, and ultimately both are willing to confront extreme potential danger.

ARTICLE 9 — *Parenting Lessons in the Interrogation Room*

Miranda Law Revisited

Miranda promises custodial suspects the right against self-incrimination, and also the right to counsel. Based upon Gault v. Arizona juvenile offenders have the same Miranda rights as their adult counterparts. In most states the juvenile's right extends to having either a juvenile officer or a parent present at the time of the interrogation process.

Juvenile Officer Role

In major city police departments juvenile officers engage in investigating both crimes committed by youths and reports of neglect or abuse. A secondary role is to be present at the time the youth has been arrested, for whatever custodial interrogation is to occur; the youth officer then adjudicates the arrestee, determining whether a court appearance, detention, or both are appropriate to the incident.

A study of the literature implies that lawmakers assume that juvenile officers act as advocates of the youth in custody, in much the same manner in which a defense attorney might if present. However, the practical application is generally that, as a member of the police department, the juvenile officer simply joins in the interrogation process along with other arresting or investigating officers. At the most, the juvenile officer might remind other interrogators to proceed in a gentle manner given the youthful status of the individual in custody. Yet they remain on the side of police.

It is also to be noted that the great latitude of the juvenile officer in the adjudication process is a strong weapon of the police to gain confessions. "People who tell the truth and are sorry get a chance to go home," is not an unusual line to hear from a juvenile officer. At the same time it is also common to hear a youth told, "Hard guys go to detention and court. Is that what you want?"

Both statements are true to the extent that a primary job of the juvenile officer is to find the thin line between the acts of a troubled child and that of a hardened youth attempting to beat the juvenile justice system. It is ironic that the safeguards provided youthful offenders are available to them, however to the extent that they wish to utilize those rights, or even understand them, these safeguards act against them. Those who wish to be safeguarded are seen as being streetwise and therefore lack the innocence likely to keep them out of detention and court.

Parental Reaction

Parents summoned to the police station by juvenile officers typically respond in one of two distinct manners. Some parents immediately urge their child to tell the truth and be honest with the police. Others angrily deny their child's involvement in the act, regardless of the degree of evidence against him/her, and almost uniformly accuse the police of unjustly involving the child in something he/she is innocent of having done.

Irony of Parental Involvement

There seems to be two clear-cut types of parents who respond to the police interrogation: those who are honest people who are shocked to learn that their child is in serious trouble with the law, and those who dislike police authority and have perhaps taught criminal behavior to their child. To the casual observer it might seem that the concerned parents would be most able to protect their child's legal interests, while the troubled child from the troubled home would likely lack for interest and legal support. In reality, the opposite exists as it applies to the juvenile suspect.

The honest, concerned parents are actually most likely to implore their child to "do the honest thing" and tell the police exactly what happened. In those instances where the child is guilty of legal wrongdoing, the result is likely to be serious legal consequences as the price paid for practicing rigorous honesty with the police.

By contrast, the parents who think poorly of the police function and middle-class society invariably blame the police for wrongly accusing their child; either the police are wrong or the alleged victim of the offense is wrong. The accused child, however, is never wrong. Thus the parents are most certain to invoke Miranda on their child's behalf.

ARTICLE 10 — *Police Response to Social Disorganization*

Social Disorganization occurs when there is a breakdown of effective social bonds and social controls in neighborhoods. Such breakdowns are frequently demonstrated by the nature of residents' usage of both the police and other social services.

<u>What the Police are Asked to Do</u>

Monday, 7:15 a.m.

A patrol car is dispatched to a public housing building on an assignment of "trouble with the daughter." Upon their arrival the officers are met at the front door by a woman in a housecoat who states that she is glad that the police have arrived as she is most worried about her daughter. Once inside the apartment the officers see a nearly dressed ten-year-old with pigtails sitting at the kitchen table. The mother folds her arms and turns toward the child stating, "Tell this girl that you will take her to jail if she doesn't eat her eggs." With that the child begins crying, and it is only after much reassurance on their part that the police convince the child that she is not going to be arrested. This prompts the mother to complain about lack of police service. After soothing everyone involved, the police leave after bringing some sense of order to a condition which essentially makes no sense.

Monday, 10:20 a.m.

Patrol officers are assigned to a call of a "sick woman" in a rundown apartment in a lower-class community. An obese woman informs the police that they need to tell her boyfriend that she feels ill and therefore not in the mood to make love to him. One of the officers matter-of-factly tells the man that it is unsafe to engage in sex so close to giving birth. Both parties begin talking at once and it is quickly determined that neither the lady of the house nor her boyfriend are of the opinion that anyone present is pregnant. The officers diplomatically respond that although nobody is pregnant, since the lady doesn't feel great, going to the hospital might be a wise move. An hour later the baby was born.

Monday, 3:43 p.m.

A call to the police was made from the local public library regarding a disturbance. Officers arrived to find that a young woman was waving a knife at the librarian while her young son stood by her side. It seems that the woman, who by now had been disarmed, was upset upon being told that she needed a library card to take out books. "How am I supposed to teach my son to f_ _ _ _ _ _ read if I can't take out books?"

In each of these case studies the subject of police intervention lacked a general awareness of basic information which most individuals possess. Note that in two cases mothers did wish for the best for their children, yet both were essentially powerless as to how to accomplish their good intentions. The case where her own pregnancy escaped the individual who had called the police does not actually deal with social service issues, but rather serves to illustrate how a generalized lack of awareness holds certain individuals back.

Crime is Normal Revisited

A theory of criminology which states that in many lower-class communities crime is an expected function of society. The extent of crime in such neighborhoods is great enough so that residents routinely see criminal acts around them.

Case Study

Police are called to a high-rise public housing building on a warm spring afternoon regarding "a woman shot." Officers find a lady sitting at the kitchen table munching on an apple while resting her head on her hand. "Ma'am, we got a call of a woman shot. Do you know anything about that?" The lady took another bite of the apple and said that she was the person who was shot. She then moved her hand away from a temple to show where a small caliber slug had entered her head.

She went on to explain that her son had shot her in the head over money. He had asked for a dollar, but the mom told him that he could take fifty cents from her purse. It was then that he warned his mom that he really did need a dollar. When she once again refused the request, the son took a .22 revolver from her purse and shot her in the head. He then took the sought after dollar before leaving.

Officers asked for a description of the shooter, which was quickly sent to other police units. "Wanted for aggravated battery and attempted murder from said address, be on the lookout for Rodger More, age 8, last seen wearing blue jeans and a yellow Snoopy T-shirt." On the way to the hospital the mother confided to the police that she was beginning to become concerned that if things continued as they were that Rodger was destined to get into serious trouble.

There are two significant aspects attached to this case study. The first issue is that individuals who are shot in the head usually go into shock due to the magnitude of the act and the potential seriousness of the injury. The mother's matter-of-fact response might be attributed to having lived at the core of a community where crime and violence are seen as a normal function of society. Having seen many previous acts of violence might have served as a conditioning agent that having been shot in the head was simply a matter of business as usual. This explains the total lack of panic on the part of the victim.

The mother's business-as-usual outlook at her young child's decision to shoot her in the head over a dollar represents another strong indication that the event was seen as not being extraordinarily unusual or violent when compared to other similar actions all around her.

The nature of police patrol work is that the only task required of officers is to answer the radio and respond to calls for service. Proactive policing, where officers inquire into a condition on their own initiative, remains voluntary in nature in that observers cannot rightly accuse anyone of ignoring an apparently stolen auto or an individual on the street carrying an illegal firearm. An officer accused of failure to respond to a situation needs only to say that their head must have been turned looking at something else.

It is common knowledge in every police department which officers engage in voluntary policing. And in the same way everyone knows who is likely to be first to arrive at "hot calls" such as robberies in progress, men shot on the street, and shots fired on the public way. Eager, self-motivated officers race to such calls for service, while others who may wish to avoid work, danger, or both may filter their risk level of confronting danger by laying back on the call. By simply driving slowly to the crime scene a given officer can assure that other officers will be there well in advance of their own arrival. Since the first to arrive at a crime scene is also most likely to actually confront the suspect, by taking one's time a fearful officer can stay far more safe.

The officers who typically arrive first at "hot calls" come to be known as "workers," while those who lay back on hot calls are often referred to by other officers as "dogs." While the percentages may differ between one police department and the next, it is probably that the "workers" make up ten percent of the work force, and "dogs" are perhaps a slightly larger percentage of fifteen to twenty percent. Thus, at least three-quarters of the patrol workforce fit in neither of the above typologies. Most officers neither "break their neck" to arrive first at hot calls, nor do they purposely move more slowly than required in order to miss the action at the crime scene. Most officers just go about their job in a workmanlike manner and do what is required in any given situation.

Comments

The fact that the most aggressive officers are known as "workers" seems to strongly suggest that the nature of patrol work does not generally call for the performance of work. Similarly, the mainstream officers who make up the majority of departments, while not "dogs" or work-avoiders, do not do a great deal of work themselves. Though they handle the assignments before them they do not take extreme steps to create more work for themselves through proactive policing.

Workers and mainstream officers assimilate smoothly, and the issues as to job functions are seldom, if ever, discussed among themselves. By contrast, the officers referred to as "dogs" are generally not a part of the police subculture society. While it is an individual officer's choice of how quickly to respond to a crime scene, those who lay back in response to a hot call may be placing their fellow officers at risk. More than once officers have been alone while involved in shoot-outs or physical encounters with dangerous individuals simply because "dogs" failed to move quickly enough to have been of help where help was much needed.

ARTICLE 13 — Drug Spots and Common Knowledge

That crime is normal is a recurring concept of criminology. Within many lower-class communities illegal behavior is as common as basketball games and kids jumping rope. When residents of such areas are asked to describe the amount and type of crime present, their responses most often are variations of saying that drug sales occur around the clock. Pick a street corner and there is drug activity.

In order to learn how true the statements are about ongoing drug trafficking, a simplistic research project was undertaken to test residents' awareness of the presence of drugs in the immediate area. However, a decision was made to ask those individuals least likely to actually be involved with drugs, the very young and the very old.

Research Method

The setting was a park district facility within a lower-class area of a major city. The park field house offers a variety of programs including dance and art classes for elementary school-age children, and also a wide variety of programs for senior citizens. The research subjects were therefore in two different age groups: Group I was made up of children fourteen years old and younger. Groups II were seniors over the age of sixty. Research thinking was that the vast majority of street drug users are within the age range

71

from mid-teens to middle age. However, the actual purpose of the research was to determine whether the presence of street drug dealers was actually a matter of common knowledge. Thus, it was decided to ask the question of those residents of an age least likely to know about the drug culture within the community.

The pair of researchers was introduced to park district users as new summer employees. Those who were questioned were first asked about a variety of community social conditions such as church denominations and locations and where the police station was situated. Finally, each was asked whether or not drugs were being sold locally on street corners, and if so, where?

The Sample

A total of forty-four children were asked about their knowledge of local drug sales. Twenty children were ages nine to twelve, the other twenty-four were thirteen- and fourteen-year-olds. Among the younger children nine were male, the other eleven were female. Among the older children fourteen were male and ten were female.

Thirty-six senior citizens were questioned, twenty males and sixteen females. All were over the age of sixty; however, no secondary classification by age was utilized.

The Results

An astounding seventy-two of eighty individuals interviewed stated that they could readily identify a nearby street corner drug operation. The breakdown by age was as follows:

Ages 9-12	Yes 18	No 2
Ages 13-14	Yes 23	No 1
Seniors	Yes 31	No 5

Research Place

The individuals questioned about drug conditions were interviewed when alone and therefore apart from peer influence. All were spoken to at the front reception desk area of the park field house. Researchers made their inquiries in a matter-of-fact tone; at no time did the researchers take notes during the interviews.

Research Follow-Up

Researchers engaged in observations of obvious drug dealing at several locations prior to the outset of the questioning. Then once the locations were stated to researchers, follow-up observations were made in an effort to confirm the information given to them.

Of the seventy-two individuals who stated that they were aware of the location of local drug dealing, a total of twenty different drug operations were mentioned in all. One drug operation was mentioned ten times, three others were mentioned six times, and four street-corner operations were mentioned four times each. Twenty-eight other drug operations were mentioned once each. Thus, a total of thirty-six drug operations were identified by very young and very old residents of the community. Researchers' observation was able to easily confirm the existence of all but four of the drug spots named by research sources. This is not to say that the other four did not exist.

Conclusion

The vast majority of those questioned did know of the existence of a currently operating drug spot. Thus it can be readily concluded that such knowledge is indeed common knowledge, and also that crime is clearly normal within that specific lower-class community. These findings are also rein-forced by the apparent fact that no less than thirty-two different street-drug operations were in operation at the time of the research. Researchers commented on the fact that within the geographic area in question there were actually far more drug spots than all other retail businesses combined.

In closing, research findings clearly disclosed that the existence and location of street-corner drug spots are indeed common knowledge within the community, even among the age groups least likely to be aware of such things.

ARTICLE 14 — Addicted Teens

Three-quarters of a century ago Edwin Sutherland said that crime and delinquency are learned in much the same manner as all lessons. Just as the particular ways of committing criminal offenses are taught and learned, so are the ins and outs of drug usage. Many adolescents and teens are exposed to drug use by older siblings. Research indicates that drug use is learned in intimate groups, often from "best friends." Others learn to get "high" at school.

One often hears parents state that "there are drugs in all schools," which doubtless is a true statement. However, not all schools tolerate drugs to invade their campuses without a good fight. In side-by-side suburbs next to one major city, the high school demographics are nearly identical in terms of graduation and dropout rates, the percentage of graduates moving on to college, and also racial composition. It is with their respective tolerance for a drug culture to exist on campus that the similarities end.

In High School A there are virtually no security guards situated within the physical plant. Perhaps not coincidentally, there are drug deals being conducted on a constant level, both in hallways and particularly in washrooms, where a great deal of drug usage also takes place. Simply put, the drug culture is allowed to exist within the institution. When a disproportionately large percentage of students left school to enter in-patient drug rehabilitation programs, the school hired a full-time drug counselor. But soon after he began openly discussing the extent of the problem, he was dismissed in what was said to be a budget cut.

High School B is located only several miles away from A and has many more students. Their security force is not large but proactive in ferreting out drug dealers and users. They actively engage in locker searches and turn over all caught, even for possession of minimal amounts of drugs, to the police. Students say that the security force absolutely will not allow a drug culture to exist on campus.

Students at both schools openly discuss the relative drug practices at the two schools. At High School A the primary drugs of choice are powdered cocaine and crack, and can be purchased inside the school at any time. At High School B where the drug culture is forced away from campus, marijuana is just about the only drug seen in or around the school.

Loss of Control

Most teens who drink do so to the point of intoxication, as learning to moderate amounts of alcohol consumed is a practice that comes with time. However, not all teens respond in the same manner once under the influence. The significant difference between the youth who can drink and get away with it, and the one who cannot, rests in the issue of loss of control. Youths who demonstrate the greatest change in personality and behavior are the ones who are most likely to wind up in rehab.

Genetics do play a role in alcohol and drug consumption among youths. An individual who has one parent or grandparent who is an alcoholic or addict has a 50% predisposition toward becoming one himself/herself. If both parents or grandparents are addicted, the predisposition is greater than 90%. Note that a predisposition simply means that if one is exposed to the substance in question, the percentages are greatly against him/her being able to become a social drinker or recreational drug user. However, if the individual with the predisposition simply never starts the process of getting high, he/she is in no way driven to making a beginning with alcohol or drugs.

Treatment Programs

In general terms alcohol/drug treatment programs deal with educational aspects of addition, centering on the concept of addiction as a disease, and thus not an issue of lack of willpower.

Time is spent explaining the concept of craving which addicts have and others do not have. Once an individual who is an addict picks up the first drink or drug, he/she simply cannot stop in the way that normal people can. Issues of how the drink or drug acts upon the addict's body is explained.

The only proven successful treatment for alcoholism and addiction is Alcoholics Anonymous. Founded in 1935 it was the first 12-Step Program, and it has grown to where 2-million individuals are currently staying clean and sober in over 120 nations by following the AA directions.

Youths in treatment programs are typically exposed to AA while still in rehab, and counselors' instructions to the patient typically include: go to meetings, get an AA sponsor, put steps in your life, and stay away from your using friends.

There can be little doubt that Alcoholics Anonymous works beautifully, however it seldom works well for teenagers. To begin with, anyone entering AA must have lost enough important aspects of his/her life to make the initial admission that he/she has a serious problem. Few if any teens have had time to get in much more trouble than a couple of arrests for DUI or other obviously alcohol-related crimes. Soon after, he/she was whisked away to treatment by his/her parents.

Meetings act as reinforcement to the alcoholic that he/she qualifies to be there. An AA sponsor is like a recovery tour guide who explains effective ways to live sober, and is also a helper in placing the twelve steps in the new person's life. Many youths make good beginnings at all of these recovery tasks, however very few youthful members of AA are either able or willing to stay away from their old using friends. For most of them it becomes a matter of "monkey see, monkey do." To the extent that they stay close to their new AA friends, they have an excellent chance of staying clean and sober. However, if someone new in recovery places himself/ herself physically alongside an individual drinking or using drugs, it is nearly inevitable that he/she too will get high. Their drinking or using "bottom" is seldom great enough to remind them that for them picking up the first one spells trouble.

Thus it is no wonder that most teens wind up returning to alcohol and drugs again until such time as they have effectively created a "new bottom" replete with more serious trouble and often far greater consequences than that which landed them in treatment initially. Unfortunately, the new trouble often moves the youth from juvenile to adult status in the criminal justice system. Other times the AA dropout graduates from misdemeanor to felony offenses, and from probated sentences to inside prison walls.

Intelligence Revisited

Criminologists have studied the relationship between intelligence and criminal activity. Such research has generally centered on weighing intelligence based on IQ testing. Observers note that IQ tests are aimed at middle-class knowledge, thus lower-class individuals do not have a frame of reference as to many of the items presented in such tests. The result may well be that lower-class individuals who may commit crimes may actually be more intelligent than their IQ test results might indicate.

The Interrogation Experience

Many times when an individual has been arrested, the police may wish to ask him/her questions in conjunction with the act. Such questioning typically centers on three issues: whether or not the suspect is involved; if so, for the suspect to incriminate himself/herself; and where others are involved in the crime, to implicate accomplices.

Admissions Weighed

The Miranda decision and countless legal observers have taken the view that it is never to the advantage of a suspect to confess or otherwise implicate himself/herself to the police. Similarly, Miranda also doubted that the suspect confessed because he/she wanted to. Rather, Miranda assumed that if it was never to the advantage of a suspect to confess,

81

those who did confess must have been forced into the act by the police.

The Dynamics of Police Interrogation

Bright police investigators understand both the facts of the criminal act and the suspect's relationship to the crime. For example, it may have been known that a robbery/murder victim always carried his money fastened by a rubber band and that he wore a certain gold chain. A suspect was later arrested carrying a roll of bills bound by a rubber band and wearing a chain, which seemingly might be proven to have been the victim's.

At that moment the suspect must weigh the probability that the police will be able to prove the above facts. To the extent that the victim can be linked to the crime, the greater the chance that the suspect will be charged and convicted.

Nearly all criminal offenders are sufficiently self-centered so that once they are convinced that the state has sufficient evidence to convict, they need to become extremely concerned with the nature of the sentence they are likely to be given.

It is one thing for a criminologist to state that it is never to the advantage of a suspect to confess; however, when one might be facing anywhere from ten to one hundred years in prison, the actual length of the sentence may hinge upon the degree to which the suspect cooperates with authorities.

The police may state, "Tell us who was with you that actually pulled the trigger, and we will tell the prosecutor that you cooperated." Such cooperation might be the difference between a death penalty case or not. Or one might be sentenced to twenty years rather than twice that amount of time. At the point that the suspect becomes convinced that he/she will be proven guilty, the intelligent choice is to engage in damage control by making the sentence as light as possible. Therefore this is the reason why so many criminal suspects make voluntary decisions to confess in the interest of reducing the specific nature of their sentence.

Criminal Suspects' Response to Free Counsel

The Miranda decision of 1966 ensured that custodial suspects were informed of their rights to both silence and to counsel. The decision took the position that it was not helpful to suspects to speak to the police, and since many suspects did ultimately confess, they must have been coerced into so doing.

Police, prosecutors, and liberal legal scholars all agreed that the Miranda decision would bring about a virtual end to custodial confessions. This was not to be the case. In fact, there was only a very slight reduction in confessions in the months and years immediately following the Miranda decision.

Almost immediately after Miranda, Richard Medalie and a group of other attorneys took up space in police stations in the District of Columbia. Their purpose was to offer free and immediate legal assistance at the time of possible police interrogation.

It is to be noted that the Miranda decision, while affording free counsel to custodial suspects, does not provide legal counsel at the time of arrest and possible interrogation. The accepted wording of Miranda includes the passage, "If you lack the financial ability to retain counsel, the court will appoint one for you and no questions will be asked until then." The practical application of the rights to counsel portion of Miranda was that in the event that a suspect wished to be represented at the time of potential interrogation at the police station, it was his/her own responsibility to arrange for a private defense attorney to respond. Otherwise the suspect would be on his/her own during the police questioning/charging process.

Based upon this set of circumstances one might assume that the custodial suspects to whom Medalie offered free counsel would have rushed to take advantage of such pro bono legal advice, however such was not the case. In fact, only seven percent of suspects facing serious misdemeanor or felony charges asked Medalie to represent them inside the interrogation room.

One logical conclusion to be taken from the suspects' general lack of interest in being represented during police interrogation is that most suspect neither fear being mistreated by the police nor do they necessarily feel that making admissions of guilt is against their best interests. To the extent that this theory is valid, then the Miranda Court greatly misjudged the actual nature of custodial interrogation.

Social Disorganization

Social disorganization is a breakdown of effective social bonds and primary-group associations that result in an inability to function within the social order, which in turn may lead to criminality. Many day-to-day life-skill tasks, which most individuals take for granted, escape certain inner-city residents. The breakdown in socialization often results in an inability to perform even the most basic tasks.

Such inabilities are sufficiently numerous that both social service agents and local merchants have responded by providing service needs which are normally routinely carried by members of mainstream society. For example, currency exchanges—called check-cashing locations in some parts of the country—have evolved to take care of certain such tasks.

The Steps in Paying a Bill

In order to pay a public utility or other invoice seeking payment, an individual must
1) Have an authorized mailbox.
2) Remove the item from the box.
3) Open the envelope.
4) Obtain a money order or write a check.
5) Place the form of payment in a return envelope.
6) Obtain a postage stamp.
7) Mail the sealed envelope.

At first glance it may seem that this discussion is designed to be an exercise in the absurd, however its intent is to demonstrate that actions which demand a series of coordinated efforts become all but impossible for certain victims of social disorganization. The task of dealing with bill payment by mail requires first the belief that the task is important, in terms of both short-range and long-term consequences. The immediate danger is that one's dwelling will be with power, heat, or water while the long-term consequence of non-payment is likely to be a negative credit report. Both of these concerns are typically learned through lessons dealing with social order. If one wishes to have electricity, one must pay for it. And the way that payment most often occurs is through the seven-step method considered.

That bill payment by mail is difficult for many inner-city individuals is highlighted by the fact that currency exchanges offer to take on this and other tasks, which are not difficult for most persons.

Not all difficulties of the socially disorganized are of their own making. For example, theft from and destruction of mailboxes is rampant in inner-city areas, particularly within high-rise public housing buildings. The mailboxes are located in the vestibule of the buildings away from normal public view. Thus the task of vandalizing the locked boxes is a simple matter. Once the mailboxes will not lock, the mail carrier will not leave the tenant's mail.

For the socially disorganized a broken mailbox creates a need to visit the local post office and show a piece of identification in order to collect their mail. For the same reasons that paying bills by mail causes difficulty, so too is it a problem to conform with other tasks such as picking up mail at the post office.

It is for these stated reasons that most states have adopted the policy of mailing public aid checks to a local currency exchange rather than to the recipient's home address. Public utility firms followed suit so that the materials required for local residents to conduct their most important business matters go through currency exchanges. Additionally, currency exchanges also issue money orders for utility bills, and mail them for payment, so that the entire process has been taken away from individuals largely incapable of doing for themselves what others are able to do so very easily.

Subculture of Violence

Wolfgang and Farracuti state that a disproportionately large percentage of homicides occur predominantly among members of certain social groups, contained to certain neighborhoods. Many homicides are linked to relatively trivial events that take

89

on a greater significance because of meanings attached to them. Violent subcultures found in lower-class communities share a value system, the conduct norms of a "subculture of violence," where pride, self-respect, dignity, and status with the community are more important than human life.

Case Study

A pair of tactical officers were perched in an abandoned building at sun-up, overlooking a street corner where a string of armed robberies had occurred. The purpose of the police stakeout was to catch the robber in the act as commuters made their way to the bus stop. The robber did not surface that morning but there was criminal activity yet to come.

An older fellow walked down the block to wait for the bus to go to work. He sat down on a fire hydrant and began reading the morning paper. Moments later, another working man walked up to the same corner. He approached the older man and explained that the fire hydrant the man was sitting on actually belonged to him. Each morning he put his foot up on that hydrant as he awaited the bus to take him to work. The fellow sitting down refused to relinquish his rights to the hydrant, which led the irate individual to pull a small automatic pistol from his lunch box and fired multiple rounds into the head of the older man who had the nerve to sit on "his fire plug."

The tactical officers quickly left their observation post and disarmed the killer. The officers then asked him just why he had killed the man, to which he responded, "Now just what are you going to do if somebody was sitting on your fire plug?" The officers responded that the case seemed to be an obvious example of justifiable homicide. The killer concurred and stated that he would simply explain himself, expecting that the judge would then let him go home.

Clearly the killer was a product of the subculture of violence identified by Wolfgang and Farracuti. The victim had slighted him by sitting on what he considered to be his fire hydrant. Certainly the act in question seems to be a classic example of what Wolfgang called a relatively trivial event. Seemingly, it was not the nature of the slight which provoked the offender, but rather more of a matter of pride and self-respect issues identified by Wolfgang. Thus, it is not so much a matter of what happens to the individual as it is how they take it.

Such incidents of drastic overreaction to perceived slights are not isolated matters in the inner city. Holiday dinners are notable for the number of individuals who are violently attacked as the outgrowth of disputes over parts of the turkey. In many such instances the offenders' view of the seriousness of the disrespect is heightened by use of alcohol or drugs.

Understanding Criminal Behavior

Overview

In many inner-city communities who has committed what crime is common knowledge among street people. Word spreads quickly and freely with criminal offenders taking credit for their exploits. Police who understand this and are also aware of the manner in which crimes are carried out may make quick work of crime solution.

Case Study

An individual from the suburbs was shotgunned to death in an inner-city area alley. The offense had taken place in the middle of the night during which time drug dealers and prostitutes are most active plying their respective trades. Clearly the murder victim had gone to the area in search of either drugs or women.

Just before noon the same day a team of investigators took to the streets, which were littered by empty beer and wine bottles, and gutters were filled with empty dope bags and used needles and syringes. Nearly each street corner had a street-walking prostitute busy waving at passing cars with her pimp standing nearby affording them whatever type of protection might be called for.

The police investigators parked their car at the curb and approached a hooker and her pimp, both of whom were known heroin addicts. The police asked the pair why the victim had been killed and who had committed the crime. Both looked at the ground, stating that they had no idea as they were not involved in that type of business. During the course of the conversation several cars slowed toward the curb to negotiate business with the prostitute before speeding away upon recognizing that she was in the company of the law.

The investigators said that they were hungry and asked the pair of street people what kind of sub sandwich they wanted for lunch. The pair looked at one another wondering just what the investigators were up to. A half-hour later the investigators returned. They set up a pair of folding chairs on the sidewalk and spread a table cloth over a small cooler, before handing the pair of street people each a sandwich and soft drink. The investigators then took off their sport coats baring their guns and handcuffs. The hooker and her pimp reluctantly accepted the lunch given them.

For the next two hours at least fifty cars slowed as if to engage the prostitute, however as the police smiled and waved their way, each prospective customer sped off. As each customer took off, the prostitute and her pimp became increasingly concerned; as long as the police scared off business, they could make no money. And with no money they could buy no heroin, and with no heroin before long they would both begin going through withdrawal. Of course, the police were aware of all of that, for that was why they were there in the first place.

Finally, the pimp approached the police asking just what it would take to get them to leave the street corner so that business might resume as normal. Moments later the investigators had the name of a pimp who had killed the victim when his prostitute signaled that he carried a large amount of cash with him. Hours later the case was solved and the offenders both charged.

In this case the police used a sense of humor and their knowledge of criminal behavior and addiction to get the information sources to become willing to tell them what they needed to know. They were most professional in their approach in that they behaved above using their authority or threats to gain their sought-after information.

ARTICLE 17 — *Criminology Reasoning Applied*

Walter Miller, a criminologist in the 1950s, stated that lower-class individuals hold certain values which are simply different than those among other social groups. Miller's list of traits seen as important to lower-class individuals follows:
1) Trouble: law-violating behavior.
2) Toughness: physical prowess, daring.
3) Smartness: ability to "con," take advantage of others.
4) Excitement: thrills, risk, danger.
5) Fate: good fortune.
6) Autonomy: independence from external issues, other restraint.

Within Miller's study of lower-class societies, its members gain status from getting in trouble as the result of breaking laws. The stigma attached to deviant behavior among other classes is not present within the lower-class experience. "Trouble" is seen as a sought-after event from which status is derived.

Toughness includes the willingness to face danger, engage in reckless and daring behaviors, and the ability to confront, fight, and successfully flee from the police. As L. Thomas Winfree points out, having a black eye is a badge of honor within lower-class society. By contrast wearing a symbol of physical combat is not seen as a positive condition within other social classes.

One of the paradoxes of criminal life is that certain individuals, who may actually have little if any formal education, are brilliant in terms of crime planning and criminal leadership. Within Miller's meaning "smartness" has to do with an ability to "con" or take advantage of others. To those who seek to con others, the intended victim's kindness is taken as weakness. Such members of lower-class society are always on the lookout for someone to take advantage of.

Excitement is often the direct byproduct of having committed a criminal act. Offenders experience an adrenaline flow during the course of criminal acts, and getaways involving foot chases or high-speed auto flights all create thrills resulting from criminal risk.

Miller states that members of lower classes often take the position that they actually have little impact on their own fate. This is why gambling and playing the lottery, both efforts of seeking good fortune, are common in such areas. This same outlook that one's destiny is out of one's own control can be taken as an explanation for much of the risk-taking involved in the criminal experience in lower-class communities. "If it's my time to get killed, it's just my time," is often overheard within this culture.

Autonomy is a desired condition to the extent that lower-class behavior is often seen as being without either rules or laws as they apply to mainstream society. Miller points out that lower classes do not reject middle-class standards. Instead, lower-class behavior is simply different, in the sense that their values have been passed along from one generation to the next.

Miller Applied to Criminal Investigation

Perhaps the work of Walter Miller more than a half-century ago might be useful in the solution of a modern-day murder investigation.

Case Study

A young woman was raped and strangled in her studio apartment. She also suffered blunt trauma wounds to the head and mutilation wounds to the rear side of her torso. Police associated a neighbor of the victim to the crime and felt that the suspect gained entrance to her apartment by stating that he needed to be paid for an order of household supplies at an hour past midnight. Eventually, the police suspect was charged and convicted of the crime.

Counsel was then retained to conduct an appeal of the conviction. At the same time an investigation seeking new evidence was established. Two new pieces of information were then discovered.

The victim had been a nursing student, and defense investigators located a classmate with whom the victim had been close. She stated that she and the victim had been in class together on three days leading up to the victim's death. Her friend stated that on the first day the victim was not herself, that it was apparent that something was bothering her. Two days later the victim seemed very scared of something, and then on the day she was to die she seemed terrified about something. Unfortunately, her friend did not see fit to ask the victim just why she was terrified. The answer to that question might have also been the answer to the crime solution.

The other important fact the defense gathered was that the victim had a woman friend who had been a neighbor in the victim's building until just before the crime. It was learned that the neighbor had a criminal background and that the victim would often visit her in her apartment. Numerous gangsters visited the woman in her apartment at which time the victim would leave and return to her own apartment.

At the center of the craft of criminal investigation is the ability to take what is known and be able to create a theory which fits the case facts. In this instance the following issues are at issue:
1) The victim was raped and murdered late at night in her apartment.
2) She had been increasingly fearful in the days leading up to her death.
3) The victim would have had occasion to come in contact with gangsters associated with her neighbor.

The first logical thought process is to establish the fact that what the victim had been terrified of during the course of the last week of her life was not that her neighbor would stop by to pick up a check for household items bought.

In the course of considering theories about what had occurred, perhaps Walter Miller's list of lower-class values might help. Under the heading of "smartness" it is said that the ability to "con" someone is to one's advantage. Suppose that the victim, who was a physically attractive young woman, had met a dangerous and violent individual while visiting her neighbor. The offender would have conned or "played" the victim to his advantage. Suppose that he began the process by asking her for a small favor, which might have been technically against the law. For the purpose of argument, perhaps he asked the nursing student to get him a sleeping pill. Once the door was open, the demands would have steadily increased for larger amounts under the threat of being turned in and barred from the nursing profession.

During the week leading up to her death the offender might have demanded something more than the victim could possibly have delivered without being placed in serious jeopardy. Thus, the victim would have been overcome with fear, yet whatever she might have considered the worst possible happening, she did not consider being killed as a result of non-compliance with the killer's demands.

Might it have happened that way? Certainly Miller's theory might hold an answer to the crime.

ARTICLE 18 — An Overview of the Police Subculture

Subcultures are generally based on shared common interests. Student athletes, criminal justice majors, criminals, and the police all gravitate toward others who are involved in the same type of activities. However, it is probable that the police subculture is among the strongest and most closely-knit subculture, due to particular aspects of their work.

An examination of the police job function illustrates well the various dynamics which come together to form the police subculture. In general terms, the police

1) See people at their worst: upset, irrational, intoxicated, angry, and belligerent.
2) Are called upon to improve conditions regardless of the situation.
3) Must move from law enforcement to service and order maintenance calls for service which creates stress.
4) Feel largely unappreciated as those they help seldom say thanks.
5) Experience much bloodshed, often that of innocent victims.
6) Come to see the world as a dark place due to the amount of crime around them.

All of these elements tend to come together to create a condition where officers observe that they know things which nonpolice could never learn. What they know separates them from all other individuals who are not the police. Similarly, the police working environment breeds an inter-dependency among officers to be there for one another, to act as both a physical and emotional safeguard.

A generation ago a criminologist named George Kirkham wrote a book entitled *Signal Zero* in which he explained about how naïve he had been before having become a policeman. He had been trained by anti-police observers who, among other things, assumed that criminals commonly accepted police authority when told what to do. On one of his first days on the street as an officer, Kirkham put his hand on a suspect's shoulder and told him to calm down. The result was that the suspect ripped the rookie cop's uniform to shreds and tried to seize his gun from him. Until then, Kirkham would never have believed that anyone would even consider an unprovoked physical attack upon the police. Kirkham also came to learn that many individuals who come in contact with the police see kindness as weakness.

To the extend that these various observations are valid, it is no wonder that the police move more and more away from mainstream society and toward one another for understanding and consolation.

Dealing with Police Administration

Though there can be little doubt that many police officers primarily trust only other officers, certainly the trust discussed herein does not extend to all members of the police family. In many research works dealing with police satisfaction, including one by Winfree and Seibel (1994), working officers clearly stated that they see the worst part of their job experience is having to deal with police supervisors and administrators. The police claim is that while officers promoted to higher ranks should fully understand the nature of police problems, most often they do not act as if they do.

One theory to support this police position is that the wrong individuals are most likely to be promoted to supervisory and administrative positions within the organization. First of all, police promotional examinations are nearly always based on questions dealing with departmental rules and regulations, and not upon actual street policing experience. Therefore, the most rigid members of the organization—those most rule-oriented, are the most likely to pass promotional examinations. It is also an unfortunate fact that within many departments politically connected officers may be promoted without concern for competency. Thus, many of the least experienced street officers are most certain to be promoted. Not only are such individuals poorly qualified to supervise and manage line officers, many are also least qualified to call upon shared common experiences as a means of empathizing with working officers who routinely face the professional hazards in question.

ARTICLE 19 — *Economics of Street Gang Culture*

Overview

Just how good a job is it to be either a member or leader of a major city street gang? Perhaps the proper beginning for such a discussion should be the consideration of a few established facts regarding street gang income.

1) The Black P Stone Nation (Chicago, 1970s) was thought to have been the first major street gang to have seized the right from white organized crime to control the street sales of heroin and cocaine. Prior to that time gang members sometimes worked as street-level dealers for the Mafia.

2) The ever-enlarging size and scope of street gangs such as the Black Disciples, Vice Lords, and Latin Kings in current gang society is equal to the seven-thousand members of the Black P Stone Nation a generation ago.

3) Since the late-1980s a major player in the gang involvement with street drugs has been the Jamaican Posse, who have controlled perhaps 40% of all crack sales in two-dozen large cities east of the Mississippi River. Posses are sometimes attributed with having been the first street gang organization to control the flow of drugs from their cities or origin.

4) The great margin of profit in the illegal drug trade stems from its wholesale

purchase in kilos or pounds. For example, kilos (2.2 pounds) of heroin are 96% pure after manufacturing. By the time it is mixed with a cutting agent such as milk sugar or quinine, user quantities on the street are only 3% pure. Therefore, the drug has been cut X 30, thus the profit margin is also times thirty.

5) How a given gang member is paid for their respective roles within the sales of street drugs is based on their relative status within the street gang structure, and the actual role they play in its being made ready for sale.

Research Method

Ten former street gang members were interviewed about their past involvement in the gang and illegal drug trade. All of the subjects were active in alcohol/drug recovery through involvement with a 12-Step Program. Their respective times clean and sober ranged from ten months to eight years. Individuals in recovery were sought out for this research in that rigorous honesty is at the core of the 12-Step recovery life. Thus, their credibility as research subjects is accepted as being extremely high.

Subject 1

A 24-year-old male, with ten months clean and sober, was an active member of a major city street gang. At the age of ten he was a "pee wee" member who began working for the gang as a bike-riding lookout for street crack dealers. It was his job to "patrol" the one-square-block area surrounding the drug spot in search of the police. When a squad car was observed approaching, he would whistle to notify the street dealers, then he would race to the corner to report on the direction of the approaching police. Dealers would then break ranks and move waiting drug buyers out of the straight-line formation usually required of them. The subject worked as a lookout for seven years and was paid anywhere between $100 and $200 per night for what amounted to six- to ten-hour tours of duty. He estimates that he averaged $50,000 annually from the age of ten on.

Subject 2

A twenty-eight-year-old male, with a year clean and sober, was an active leader of a major city street gang from the age of twelve to twenty-two when he went to prison for a gang-related shooting over drug trade boundaries. Income varied according to his role in the purchase of dealer amounts. He once made $20,000 in one deal alone. He was in charge of passing drugs along to lower-ranking gang members who sold crack on street corners. He estimates that he made about $70,000 annually for his limited involvement several times a year.

Subject 3

A thirty-year-old male, with a year clean and sober, was a warlord for a major city street gang. He profited from his own buying and selling of street drugs, which his gang status allowed him to do. Money was not shared with the gang, nor were gang members organized in his dealing. He made an average of $30,000 per year by buying crack from a wholesaler and passing it along to young gang members to sell on the street. He had no income from his position as warlord, which meant that he made decisions as to violent actions against rival gang members.

Subject 4

A twenty-four-year-old male, with two years clean and sober, was a member of a major city street gang. He was paid 10% of the value of the crack he sold on a street corner. An average day involved the sale of $15,000 to $20,000 in user amounts of five to ten rocks at a time at $10 a rock. He typically worked six-hour shifts. It is to be noted that this street corner location operated around the clock, thus the estimation is that the corner averaged nearly $80,000 a day. The subject thus made $1,500 a day, or $525,000 annually based on having worked 350 days a year.

Subject 5

A thirty-two-year-old male, who has been clean and sober for four years, was a leader of a major city street gang and made no formal income except from whatever crimes he planned and carried out. The gang was involved in drug dealing but on a highly independent manner. He estimates that he might have averaged $1,000 a month from thefts and dealing user amounts of drugs.

Subject 6

This 27-year-old male has been in recovery for just over a year. He was an active member of a large well-known major city street gang, which was involved in shakedowns of drug dealers and the sale of drugs within a public housing complex. He transported drugs for the gang and sold user amounts within the building where he lived. For all of this he never was paid more than a few hundred dollars at a time.

Subject 7

A 47-year-old male, who has been in recovery for nearly ten years, was a gang leader in charge of collecting daily fees from local drug dealers for protection. He typically collected as much as $100 from each of a hundred dealers. For having collected some $10,000 a day he was paid about that same amount per month.

Subject 8

This 24-year-old male was a leader of a suburban street gang with affiliation to major city counterparts. He has been clean and sober for about a year. The gang waged war with rivals and sold user amounts of drugs in their turf area. He never was paid by the gang for his actions. Whatever money he made was the result of his buying and selling small quantities of drugs.

<u>Subject 9</u>
This 33-year-old male has been clean and sober for three years. He was an upper-level decision-maker of an Asian street gang. He bought kilos of heroin from African-American gangs and cut and sold the heroin to local retail street dealers. He made millions of dollars over a five-year time period.

<u>Subject 10</u>
A 37-year-old member of the same Asian gang discussed above has been clean and sober for over a year. He was a street dealer in that organization and made over $50,000 a year for several years.

Research findings conclude that street gang drug sales is far more a matter of being a part of a major criminal organization than being about fighting with gang rivals and other behaviors commonly associated with street gang life. Most, but not all, street gang members do profit from their involvement with drugs related to their gang affiliation.

Editor's Note: The following two articles on the Black P Stone Nation and the Jamaican Posse were co-authored by George Seibel and Ronald A. Pincomb, New Mexico State University. Both articles were initially published in Criminal Organizations Journal, in Summer 1994 and Summer 1999 respectively.

ARTICLE 20 — From the Black P Stone Nation to the El Rukns: Reflections of a Chicago Street Cop

Introduction

    This paper is purely unscientific in nature and written from the perspective of a street cop who lived this experience on a daily basis for a period of over three years' time. The incidents are real, the perspectives are mine.

    The people and the locale comprise a place I have often referred to as the "insanity belt," and for good reason. It was a place where human life was viewed as worthless. Such attitudes cause significant problems for the police for, as many a cop has learned, you can't take something from a person who has nothing.

Setting

    The occurrences depicted took place in an area of urban decay, of buildings seemingly held up by the graffiti, and of public housing projects, vertical holding places for humanity—normally twelve stories high with ten to fifteen apartments per floor. The only lasting businesses were those aimed at instant gratification: bars, fast foods, cleaners, record shops, and dope houses.

The community was marked by far-reaching social disorganization. Conflicts on every possible level, among all ages were ever present; a place where people called the police in the hopes of forcing their children to eat their breakfast cereal.

The area was ninety-nine percent Black. Over ninety percent were public aid recipients. Another ninety-five percent of all births were out of wedlock. And most importantly, it was a place where crime and violence was normal.

The Beginnings of the Blackstone Rangers

In 1962 the premiere street gang on the South Side of Chicago were the Black Disciples. Though informally organized, they were far stronger in both numbers and power than the numerous upstart gangs, which were "here today and gone tomorrow." During the spring of that year a group of Disciples attacked a second-grader by the name of Bennie Fort. Crime on the city's South Side would never be quite the same for the next three decades.

Bennie Fort went home and told his older brother, Jeff, what had taken place. Jeff in turn walked down the block from his home to the corner of Sixty-fifth and Blackstone, where five of his friends were hanging around the mailbox. Within the next hour's time the Blackstone Rangers were born. Present on

112

the street corner that night with Fort were Mickey Cogwell, a pudgy and soft looking kid, Eugene "Bull" Hairston, and Clarence "Cashoshe" Torry. Hairston was a tall, rangy type who, it is said, had some genuine basketball skills. Both Jeff Fort and Torry were small, slight and dark complected, unimposing until you gazed into their ruthless eyes—eyes which told you that their bodies were flowing with canned evil where blood might have otherwise been.

The next day Fort and Torry went to the pool hall where the Black Disciples gathered. Armed with .9 mm semi-automatics, the pair let fly with 28 rounds. Three died and ten others were perforated.

After tossing their weapons along the way, Fort and Torry stood in front of the same mailbox as they had the night before, awaiting the arrival of the police. They were not disappointed.

Despite having been identified in a line-up by many victims and witnesses, the pair were released by the police without charge.

It seems that Fort and Torry had an alibi; a good one. A respected grocery storeowner had told the police that the suspects had been with him in his store at the time of the shooting. His word was seen as far more preferable than that of a bunch of gang members. Several hours after the release of Fort and Torry, another release took place. The storekeeper's wife was released from where she had been held by Hairston and

Cogwell in the basement of an abandoned building.

This first incident of violence had all of the earmarks which was to become Fort's method of operation—defiant flair.

An observer might well raise the issue that Fort risked apprehension by first kidnapping the shopkeeper's wife. What if he had confided in the police? I myself pondered such questions countless times during the three years I was to play "cat and mouse" with Fort and the Stones. But the answer was always the same and totally clear cut.

Jeff Fort had a magnetism predicated on immense evil. Clarence Torry had much the same quality. People simply knew that there was no limit to their potential for treachery. Years later I was to have a conversation with a Stone leader by the name of Alan "Black Jesus" McTush. Black Jesus had just been shot on Fort's order because he had bungled an extortion plot. In but a few words he told the story of what Jeff Fort was all about.

"When The Rat (Fort) threaten me I ain't never afraid of what he say he gonna' (do). Whatever he got way in the back of that mind far, far worse than anything he say."

By the Fourth of July of that same year (1962) there were over one hundred Stones packing that same street corner, by now wearing the label of the gang, red berets. Fort's open defiance of both the police and the Black Disciples was quickly attracting the most anti-social deviants in the area ranging in age from ten to well into their thirties.

The Stones' membership tripled in each of the succeeding three years, so that by 1965 the Stones were nearly one thousand strong. During 1965 Fort embarked upon the beginning of enforced recruitment. He wanted numbers and he got them. The tactic was simple: become a Stone—or die.

Several did say "no," and they not only died, but the Stones left absolutely no doubt whatever as to who was responsible. Each body was invariably propped up against the mailbox on the corner of Sixty-fifth and Blackstone.

At the same time the Black Disciples, led by twenty-six-year-old Frank Barksdale, were no shrinking violets. They, too, began involuntary recruitment and had grown to nearly 1,500 strong. Not unexpectedly, Jeff Fort had a better idea: the Stones went city-wide. Hoards of Stones, often one thousand strong, headed into every part of the city where Black street gangs functioned. Summits with the various gang leaders occurred. The word was always the same from Fort: "Come with me or I'll wipe out your band of a couple hundred without working up a sweat."

Some came out of fear but most jumped at the chance to become Stones. Those of lesser evil were mesmerized by the force and aura of Jeff Fort.

By late-1965 the Blackstone Rangers had become the Black P Stone Nation. Jeff Fort now had complete and total control of well over seven thousand of the most dangerous gangsters in the City of Chicago.

Black P Stone Nation, Circa 1968

Segments of the Stones operated throughout Black communities, in the infamous Cabrini-Green Housing Projects on the Near-North Side and all the way to the southern-most portion of the city. These satellite Stones each operated under their own president with tactical assistance and firepower, when needed, from Fort and Torry.

The 1965 coalition had a very direct impact upon the extent of power now held by the original Stones. For two miles to the north had been a thousand or so very crazy dudes who had been members of various extremely dangerous, but disorganized gangs. Now under the direction of the Stones, many of these people "blossomed" into their own in the game of treachery. Brothers Alan and Sammy Knox, Anthony "Sundown" Sumner, and Stanley Cochran were all to play vital roles in the tyranny to come.

With this growth came a move of Stone Headquarters from the Woodlawn area and their original street corner to East Forty-seventh Street, in the Kenwood-Oakland community.

During this time Jeff Fort began seeing the potential for evil deeds beyond fighting the Black Disciples. There was no money in shooting rival gang members.

Figure 1. Evolution of "The El Rukns"

BLACKSTONE RANGERS
↓
BLACK P STONE NATION
(Late 1965)
↓
EL RUKN SUNNI MUSLIMS
(Jeff Fort aka Prince MALIK)

Fort's first effort at putting his power to work was by charging people attending school; a quarter a day in grammar schools and a dollar a day in high schools.

Before you scoff at the notion that this is organized crime, I suggest you view the accompanying chart and look at the estimated annual take from this endeavor. (Before you do that take a guess at the dollar amount.)

At about this time a white minister from a church in nearby Hyde Park (home of the University of Chicago) began speaking out publicly, taking the position that Fort and the Stones were merely victims of their environment and a racist police force. Upon meeting the minister, Fort immediately knew that each of them had something the other wanted desperately. The minister had a church in which the Stones could hide their arsenal, and Fort had more young boys at his beck and call than the minister could ever hope to love.

Thus began the first of many attempts to legitimize the Black P Stone Nation.

Historical Perspective

These years marked the height of liberalism in our nation. During this period of dissent the Black Panther Party took responsibility for the murder of countless police officers across the country. Among the many active supporters of the BPP was Jane Fonda, and the University of California at Berkeley. Within such an atmosphere it is therefore not surprising that Jeff Fort found himself sharing Black Power handshakes with the University of Chicago's president.

Fort came to realize that he could talk liberal-ese with the best of them, condemning "The Establishment" for the violence among his people (this is taken to mean Blacks generally as opposed to the Stones).

The Grant Fiasco

Fort learned that through a neighborhood organization, The Woodlawn Organization (TWO), the Stones might apply for federal funding for a program to give gang members job skills. Through the TWO the Black P Stone Nation did gain a grant in the amount of one million dollars. Here is how Fort ran the program.

1) Lower-level leaders of the Stones were hired as program instructors—though most were illiterate.

2) Stone enforcers recruited young members of the community to enroll as students.

Students were paid $125 per week to be a part of the program.

3) Each Friday when the student's checks were disbursed, Stone enforcers were waiting outside the door. Students would endorse over their checks and be given a $20 bill in return. The remainder became profit to the Stones.

Members of the Chicago Police Department became aware of this scam, which constituted state violations including felony intimidation in addition to countless federal fraud charges. Chicago Police then documented these activities and presented factual data to the FBI. Federal authorities stated that they would act upon the evidence—which was strong.

Some two years later Fort was called before a U.S. Senate hearing. He strutted in, smirked, scared the hell out of a number of already nearly dead politicians, and then walked out. He was later found guilty of having embezzled $7,500 (the June 1968 student payroll), and sentenced to seven years in prison, 1970-76.

Fort named Clarence Torry in charge of the Nation during the term of Fort's confinement. In March of 1970 Mickey Cogwell returned from a stint in prison, intent upon assuming Fort's position. Three days later Cogwell was found dead in a vacant lot on the 4700 block of South Ingleside. His throat was slit ear to ear in a series of twenty-one separate cuts, indicating that he had been sliced a half-inch at a time, denying him the dignity of dying quickly. He was apparently kept alive for many hours, bleeding to death a trickle at a time. In keeping with Fort's defiant style, Cogwell was left directly across the street from the residence of the Stones' general in charge of internal matters. There was to be no doubt that Cogwell had been killed by his own. With each of the hundreds of murders, before and after, there was always a clear message to be felt throughout the community.

The Police

Authorities made an initial error in underestimating the dynamic Fort. But then, few might have guessed at his charisma and uncanny leadership abilities. In any case we who watch police administration closely invariably expect bungling and are seldom, if ever, disappointed.

At the same time on the street level the police were experiencing more than a few victories. Members of both the Prairie Avenue District tactical team and the Gang Intelligence Unit were taking sawed-off shotguns away from younger Stones on nearly a daily basis. Juveniles were charged locally but adults were turned over to ATF to be charged under federal statutes.

In the summer of 1970 the Main 21 (see Organization Section) made a decision to respond to intense police attention: They would put a "hit" on a Gang Intelligence officer.

Officer James Alfano was riding in the back seat of a 3-man squad car in the area of Sixty-third and Stony Island when shots rang out from atop a seven-story hotel. A round fired from the carbine entered the rear cushion next to where he sat, hit a spring, and entered his back. He died of that wound less than an hour later.

Street cops from throughout the South Side with knowledge of the Stones were immediately summoned. Raiding parties ranging from six to eight members each were organized to pick up all members of the Main 21 (who had made good their escape from the hotel).

What follows are a very few words as to how you establish target locations when conducting raids.

1) Hit each dwelling listed as an address given on a party's criminal history sheet.

2) Hit every address given for every person with whom your target has ever been arrested.

3) Most street cops know women in the target's life. Their houses get hit too.

You may ask if the above-listed factors constitute probable cause to search. Obviously not. But when a policeman is killed nobody seems to care about constitutional constraints. Doors are simply kicked in and shotguns put in someone's mouth. Is it illegal? Sure it is. Is it morally wrong? Today, detached as I am, writing this with a pipe in my mouth, I say certainly it is objectionable on many levels. But that is just how it is.

One of those located and arrested that night was a middle-level hit man named Casari Marsh. He talked with a promise that the States Attorney's Office would give him seed money and a new identity in return for his story and later, his courtroom testimony.

Yes, he had been there. No, he had not pulled the trigger. The carbine and the scope had come from a twelve-year-old Stone who got it in a burglary. It all checked out. Seven were charged with murder. They were all released after the charges were dropped. Casari got lonesome for his girl friend. He and she met for a rendezvous in the Mercury Hotel in March, 1971. They left the hotel in His and Hers body bags. No witness equals no trial.

Terror for Profit

By early 1971 the Stones, under the direction of Clarence Torry and let by Fort's instructions from prison, began expanding their extortion practices. Their new target was to be prostitution.

On any given night in the area between Thirty-fifth and Forty-seventh Streets, and from Cottage Grove east to Lake Michigan (one mile) there would be anywhere between 100 to 150 streetwalkers plying their trade. Stone enforcers quickly got the word to both pimps and the ladies themselves that it would henceforth cost each hooker $50 a day to work the street and stay alive.

Soon after a ninety-pound heap resembling a large blob of strawberry preserves was found beneath a window of the Sutherland Hotel—on the very corner where the Stone leaders could be found every day of the week. The person on the pavement beneath the window had been a hooker with the very cool street name of Martha Vandella. She had resisted the notion of paying $50 a day to be able to do what she had always done. In death she served as a very vivid reminder to all of her counterparts working the street—pay or die.

Seven Stones were arrested and charged with her murder in what I must admit was a bit of clever, if borderline illegal, police work. The murder smacked of a group of second-tier enforcers. They were all located together on the street and arrested. All seven were assembled in the lockup and fingerprinted. The leader of the crew was then separated then later returned to where the others sat. The cell door was then opened and the leader told that he was free to go. He was puzzled but did leave.

The others were thus left with the clear implication that their leader had bought his freedom by talking. Two of the crew then did talk. Their account of events was in line with physical evidence and previous police discoveries. Prior to having been tossed out a sixth-story window to her death, Martha Vandella's attackers had cut off her nipples and forced a quart glass bottle up her vagina.

Though all seven attackers were charged with the gruesome murder, Jeff Fort and the Stones once again won that segment of the ongoing war. The Stones posted cash bonds totaling over $300,000 to release six of the killers from custody. The following dawn all six were found shotgunned at Thirty-ninth and Drexel Blvd., directly in front of the gang headquarters. The seventh member of the act, Willie McLillie, was stabbed to death in his cell of Cook County Jail. This time Fort's message was a warning not to get "slicked" by the police.

The same day in which the fallen Stones were killed, my partner and I stopped on Forty-seventh Street to chat with Clarence Torry. He commended us (my partner, Paul Carroll, and I) for our cunning, pointing out that his way and our way of thinking were similar in many ways. He then offered each of us a thousand dollars a week to lay off of the Stones (this was at a time when my annual police salary was $8,000).

We thanked him for the extreme compliment, stating that our activities apparently had him worried more than a little. He allowed himself an economical and evil laugh before saying that we were little more than a nuisance to him, like "flies in the king's parlor."

In many ways he was correct. Despite our obsessive efforts the truth was that up to that point we had accomplished little more than a continuous denting of their armor. But it was those efforts by thirty or so street cops that prevented the Stones from having free rein.

A Note

The only way in which one can successfully police a community is by developing an understanding of its people—primarily its criminal element—and the only effective way of developing such an understanding is to talk to those persons. The nature of my relationship with the Stone was one of mutual respect. That they were superb at what they did is obvious. They in turn both feared and respected what this band of young street cops did on a daily basis toward destroying their criminal empire.

It was a game, one of life and death, of good and evil. A game where only one team was required to adhere to rules. Both sides understood how its opponent went about their business. We did everything possible to get people to talk to us—to tell us things we could take to court. In turn, the Stones kept the level of terror sufficiently great to prevent people from talking to authorities.

Perhaps sharing a personal incident with the reader will best illustrate what it was like having been a street cop during that time. When my ex-wife filed her divorce complaint she correctly charged that I knew the names of over 2,000 gang members but didn't know who my next-door neighbors were.

Narcotics Extortion

In September of 1971 my partner and I were shooting the breeze with a street-walking prostitute between her servicing her "tricks." She lamented the fact that the cost of living was rising. Not only was she forced to pay the Stones daily protection money, but now the price of her heroin had gone up two dollars a bag. My partner and I thought this strange in light of the fact that the drug was plentiful at that time. An investigation was in order.

John Brennan was the heroin expert on our tactical team. His network of addict-informants was extensive. Within hours Brennan had confirmed that the price had gone up on heroin to defray a newly instituted street tax imposed by the Stones. Several days later we were able to piece together the facts as to a confrontation between the Stones and the Outfit, Chicago's lone supplier of heroin.

Early one evening my partner and I responded to a call of "a carload of white men in a black Olds with guns at Forty-seventh and Drexel." We assumed that the dispatcher had gotten it wrong. He must have meant to say, black men in a white Olds. But sure enough, less than a minute later we had curbed the car. Inside it were four "Outfit-types," each carrying a .25 automatic. To our joy one was outfitted with a silencer—a federal charge. None of the four arrested would talk, not even a name, but it was a simple matter of waiting for the return of fingerprints.

We learned that the call to the police about guys with guns had been made from a public phone from the drugstore at Forty-seventh and Drexel—the heart of Stone turf. A short trip to police headquarters later we listened to the recording of the call. The voice of the caller was clearly that of a 13-year-old Stone enforcer by the name of Jeffrey Jarvis.

It was obvious that the Outfit guys must have just concluded a conversation with the Stones prior to the call to police having been made. That conversation could only have been about one thing—a warning against shake-downs by Stones of heroin dealers. The fact that the Stones had set up the Outfit guys for arrest was a clear indication that the Stones were not buying the Outfit's brand of terror.

Evil is a relative term. Within the criminal milieu there are many degrees of "bad." Clearly, the traditional organized crime organization was impotent in the eyes of the Stones.

That such was the case became fully evident the following morning. Two white men were found on the doorstep of the Survivor's SAC on Taylor Street, the headquarters of the Outfit. Both men had been shot-gunned to death, each had their penis severed and placed in their mouth. Clarence Torry and the Stones had sent the Outfit a gift and a message—the shakedown of heroin dealers would continue.

The Outfit was helpless against the Stones and had they taken an objective look at the facts, they would have realized it. At maximum strength the Chicago organized crime family may have been some two hundred strong. And at least half of those were elderly leaders, themselves incapable of waging war other than by pushing buttons. The simple fact is that the Outfit mistakenly assumed they could elicit fear among the Stones for no other reason than that fear was their product. Their error was in their lack of understanding of the Stones. Had he wished to do so, Clarence Torry could have ordered literally hundreds of thirteen-year-olds with guns into the Taylor Street area, blowing away virtually everyone in sight. If shootouts with the Black Disciples were considered recreational activity, then popping a handful of middle-aged white men with soft bellies would have been a day at the beach.

The Outfit now had greater concerns than the Stones simply charging protection money to street dealers. How long would it be before the Stones seized wholesale delivery rights from them? The correct answer was "very, very soon."

It was soon learned that the two men the Stones had killed and left on the Outfit's doorstep were gunrunners from Arkansas. The Stones burned them after they had delivered over a hundred stolen shotguns and rifles. We were able to piece together that this hit had been the artistry of Stanley Cochran, their chief enforcer, but we were never able to prove it.

In order to truly understand just how treacherous the Stone were, we must grasp the notion that these other criminal elements; street gang rivals, organized crime, and southern gunrunners were themselves extremely dangerous elements in their own right. Yet the Stones swatted each away as mere pesky flies.

Income

By the beginning of 1972 the Stones were realizing immense profits through the extortion of school children, prostitutes, and heroin dealers. Virtually all of this money went, as one would expect, to the organization's leaders. To this point the young guns—those responsible for routine violence—were rewarded to the tune of $200 per gang killing.

Figure 2. Total Annual Income	
School	$1,014,000.00
Prostitution	910,000.00
Heroin	1,190,000.00
Total	**$4,114,000.00**

The thinking was that the younger members should be thrown an additional financial bone. It was therefore decided that the younger faction would be allowed to extort protection money from area merchants under the direction of a Main 21 leader named Sammy "Little Dog" Knox. These shakedowns varied from $50 a week from corner groceries to several hundred from franchise restaurants (it is notable that the only failed McDonalds franchise to that date was in the midst of Stone territory).

Merchants

It is estimated that the younger faction of the Stones took in some $250,000 annually which they were allowed to divide among themselves.

It is in this area that the police were most successful in gaining prosecutions. Though the actual extortion enterprise was under the direction of sufficient controls, it was not always possible to keep 14-year-olds from flashing thousands of dollars about. In many instances the police would conduct field interrogations among this set and were able to make legitimate arrests on a variety of levels. In many such instances the arrestees would have huge sums of cash on their persons. This money would then be inventoried as prisoner's property. Fearing a major investigation, the Main 21 ordered those arrested to take no steps toward recovering their money.

In other instances the police would bargain with the arrestees, allowing them to keep their cash in return for information about other Stone activities.

The Revolving Door

Jeff Fort returned from serving his time on the federal embezzlement charges. The police got someone to talk about merchant extortion and Sammy Knox was sent away. Stanley Cochran, who had personally killed nearly 200 people, got caught with a "blazing gun," literally running into the side of our squad car after having pumped eight rounds into a troublesome heroin dealer. Stanley has since become a successful portrait painter in Pontiac State Penitentiary where he is a life-long resident.

In all, by the end of 1973, fifteen members of the Main 21 were incarcerated. Clarence Torry was one of the six never to have been nailed.

Birth of the El Rukns

In 1982 Jeff Fort was back inside a federal institution, this time for his masterminding of a cocaine conspiracy. The DEA was able to build a case on him by overlooking two or three murders on the part of the dealer they "flipped" to testify against Fort.

It was at the outset of this prison term that Fort became Prince Malik and the Black P Stone Nation was transformed into the El Rukns. Contrary to popular writings, the El Rukns were not a prison gang at their inception, nor were they ever. Fort came up with the religious angle out of need. He and the Stones had invested a literal fortune in real estate properties on the South Side of Chicago. Most were held in blind trusts, but once the federal authorities finally became interested in the Stone, they had little difficulty in establishing true ownership.

Within this context Fort realized that he would become tax exempt if he became a religious leader. It was a simple as that.

Using his genius he created a code language, and his spooky and charismatic appearance was a perfect march for his new outfits—turbans and dashikis.

Under the new name, many of the old Main 21 members were released from incarceration at virtually the same time. They simply became "generals" instead of members of organized crime.

In virtually all other respects it was business as usual. The graffiti in the same community simply changed to El Rukn. During the years between the late-1970s and the beginning of the next decade Fort had taken over heroin distribution from the impotent Outfit and had also become heavily involved in the cocaine trade as it grew like wildfire.

By then Fort had received national attention, not only from the media but from far-flung criminal enterprises as well. Eventually Moammar Gadhafi sought out Fort to plant a few bombs and do a rocket-launcher number on behalf of Libya. By then the FBI had broken the El Rukn code and had tapped the pay phone from which he made calls from the Texas federal penitentiary where he was housed. Thus that plot was cracked before consummation.

In 1988 the FBI learned that Anthony "Sundown" Sumner and Trammell "Trim"

Davis had killed a dope dealer named Willie Bibbs on orders from Fort. Both Sumner and Davis had been with Fort since the early 1970s as Main 21 members. However, their loyalty to Fort was over. The offer from the FBI of ten years for the killing with new identities upon release was too good to pass up.

Black P Stone Nation From
An Organized Crime Perspective

The Stones met all of the criteria of an organized crime enterprise in that they had excellent direction, an elaborate hierarchy, and sold terror. Their annual income as far back as 1972 was formidable, if not so when compared to traditional organized crime.

However, the terror the Stones created was far different than the covert acts of traditional organized crime. An entire generation of poor people forced to live on the South Side of Chicago were forced to live a truly unendurable existence, in a place that was unsafe for everyone from toddlers to senior citizens, a place where no such amount of urban violence has ever occurred before or since. Beyond the scope of crime for profit the Stones were also involved in most every form of criminal endeavor known to man. Wearing of the red beret constituted carte blanche for taking whatever they wanted—everything from merchandise in stores to women. Virtually every resident was in some way touched by their reign of terror.

In conclusion, no other criminal enterprise has ever influenced the quality of life for area residents to the extent of the Black P Stone Nation. And though sinister, few men have possessed the brains, guile, and leadership abilities of Jeff Fort.

ARTICLE 21 — *A View of the Jamaican Posse: A Successful and Anonymous Criminal Organization*

Overview

In the middle-1980s the U.S. Attorney's Office called Jamaican Posses responsible for forty percent of the crack trade in this country. Nearly a decade later the Bureau of Alcohol, Tobacco and Firearms and the Drug Enforcement Administration estimated that they control no less than fifty percent of all illegal drugs in thirty major cities in the eastern half of the nation.

This data begs the question of how posses might have become so successful a criminal organization and at the same time remained almost totally anonymous apart from only the most enlightened law enforcement officials.

Observational research was undertaken in an attempt at gaining answers to this dilemma, the results of which are then compared against the previous literature.

Introduction

This decidedly unscientific research project began with a passing comment of a young friend of mine who is a recovering addict who stated that the street where he lives was ". . . swarming with Jamaican Posse crack." As criminologists and former police detectives, Ron and I jumped at the opportunity to see first hand whether their operation was in keeping with the limited literature at our disposal.

Our research method was the same as it would have been during our police days; we would ask people questions and observe the alleged crack operation. We would then match our findings against the literature.

Section I of this article is a historical overview of Jamaican Posse garnered from the scholarly literature, law enforcement reports, and media works. Section II is a presentation of what we found, while Section III offers an analysis of findings and a comparison of findings against the prior literature.

SECTION I
Historical Perspective

Jamaica is an extremely impoverished nation where corruption and violence has long been associated with its government. Each neighborhood in Kingston, the nation's largest city, is typically entirely supportive of one political party of the other. The opposing parties both made use of armed political enforcers to intimidate voters and eliminate rival party members.

These political gunmen were the same persons who typically sold marijuana and routinely committed acts of armed robbery and other violent crimes. However, their allegiances and gang ties were tightly connected to political affiliations.

In the 1980 election there were over 750 violent deaths directly attributable to political gunmen. This condition proved to be an embarrassment, if not a true concern, to party

136

leaders who therefore encouraged their hired guns to leave the country (Miami Herald, 1992).

Entire neighborhoods of former political gunmen left their homes and migrated to New York City, entering the United States by use of fraudulent documents as migrant workers and on temporary visitors' visas. They then quickly went about the business of establishing themselves as dealers of highly potent marijuana from their own nation.

Each of four separate and opposing groups from Jamaica became active in gun battles with existing New York City street gangs for the right to ply their criminal trade. Quick to shoot first and negotiate much later, the posses exhibited such an intense willingness to act out violence that they were able to carve out "drug turf" where only the most notorious street gangs had operated previously.

The four initial groups in New York City were the Shower, Dunkirk, Jungle, and Spangler Posses. By 1982 the posses had seized control over nearly all of the marijuana sold in New York City, forcing them to begin purchase of crops from Texas, Arizona, and other areas to keep up with demand for the product.

During this time each posse remained politically intact with all of its members being trusted associates from a particular area of Jamaica. As of 1982 the Spangler Posse was the largest and most powerful; however, a subsequent drug war with the Dunkirks cost them control of their New York City drug turf. The Dunkirk Posse and the Spanglers were initially of approximately equal size, about 2,000 members each; however, the Dunkirks imported another 1,000 members from Jamaica. At the same time it was estimated that the Jungle Posse had some 700 members while the Shower Posse was slightly larger (New York Times, 1984).

A Shift to Cocaine

By late 1982 numerous "splinter posses" spun off from the initial four and set out to ply their violence in numerous cities, primarily on the East Coast of the United States. At approximately the same time Jamaican Posses entered into the illegal cocaine industry, which provided a far greater profit margin than marijuana. During the time in which the splinter groups were becoming established, two major changes took place. For the first time posses were no longer founded upon old political lines dating back to Jamaica. And also for the first time, persons other than Jamaicans were allowed entry into their organizations.

As splinter posses moved into new cities, previously existing street gangs or other criminal organizations proved to be no match for the Jamaican Posses, either in terms of pure numbers, or in a willingness to act out violence. By the end of the 1980s there would be some 70 different posses with a total of more than 14,000 members.

Organization

Jamaican Posses are not highly structured organizations in that specific job functions are seldom, if ever, assigned at the upper echelon level. For example, no one person is specifically in charge of obtaining kilo quantities of cocaine for a specific posse. Rather, as the need for that function comes about, a member of the ranking order simply will assume the task.

In general terms posses are comprised of three levels of hierarchy: ranking members, middle echelon, and workers. Day-to-day operations are managed by middle echelon members who act as overseers. Ranking members seldom live in the outlet cities where the posse is operating. They are far more likely to reside either in New York City, Miami, or in source cities for the illegal drugs. Leaders visit outlet cities only when serious problems arise. All high ranking and middle-echelon members are Jamaican, and most are from the same neighborhoods in the home country.

Workers may be younger members recruited from Jamaica but are more often local residents from the outlet city, often former members of defeated street gangs. It is to be noted that in smaller and mid-sized cities drug trafficking may have been in the hands of gangs of fifteen or fewer members. Clearly, organizations of such size were of no match for the numbers or the violence of the posses. Once a posse has seized control of drug operations in a given city, defeated gang members gladly perform a variety of low-level functions such as street sales, transporting drugs, and acting as "look-outs."

This lack of organization has actually acted to the advantage of posses in terms of law enforcement intervention. Police called to investigate a shooting or murder involving Jamaicans invariably found no concrete evidence of an established organization present in their city. Law enforcement officials would therefore dismiss the act as random in nature, thus allowing the posse to continue their activities unnoticed. This loose organizational structure also insolates the upper-echelon members from the organization's ongoing criminal endeavors as they are often thousands of miles away from the host community.

Targeting of Cities

In such cities as New Haven, Connecticut, and Gary, Indiana, the largest and most violent street gangs are comprised of fewer than 50 members. Organizations of this size are obviously no match for a posse of perhaps three to ten times as large. In some instances the posse uses guns and violence to quickly seize control of narcotics in a new host city. Other times they easily entered into working relationships with established street gangs. Such is thought to be the case in Chicago where intelligence gathering indicates that the Striker Posse is aligned with the powerful Black Disciples, who provide the posse with enforcement and street dealers (Chicago Crime Commission, 1990).

Once again there appears to be a lack of organization as to the actual choice of cities to be taken over by posses. Jamaicans have moved in on narcotics trafficking in areas where they were ordered to stand trial and where they had visited on vacation. In such instances posse members simply established that the market for illegal drugs was present and the competition weak, and within a matter of days were in full operation.

Drug Trafficking

Jamaican posses moved successfully from the smuggling and sale of marijuana to cocaine and were therefore at the forefront of the crack explosion. At the outset of their cocaine and crack sales, posses controlled the drugs from point of purchase all the way to street distribution. During that time law enforcement officials had made no large seizures of cocaine or crack from posses. However, as demand increased, Jamaicans have taken on the role of mid-level suppliers for a specific geographic region. With this new role it is no longer unusual for large seizures to be made from Jamaican Posse workers. Operations of up to 10 kilos per week have been dismantled by the police; however, ranking members and middle-echelon members routinely have escaped apprehension.

Size and Scope of Jamaican Posses

It is estimated that 14,000 active members are involved in 85 posses operating in the United States and Canada. Posses are responsible for at least 25% of the illicit drugs sold in approximately 35 cities. This fact tends to remain a well kept secret due largely to the low profile that posse leaders maintain. Moreover, the self-contained nature of posses made it nearly impossible for covert infiltration of the organizations by police operatives.

Posse Violence

Jamaican posses have been successful in the takeover of illegal drug turf in the United States due to their relatively large numbers as compared to local street gangs, and to a greater extent, due to their unquestioned willingness to act out violence.

Initially, most posse killings were in the interest of taking over control of drug turf. Subsequent to their successful takeovers in such cities, killings continue in response to would-be challenges by other organizations. Jamaican posses also use extreme methods in killing those who betray their organizations. The firing of 30 or 40 rounds by use of multiple weapons has come to be virtually a trademark of posse murders. Torture and dismemberment are routine posse responses to acts of disloyalty within their own organization.

Law enforcement officials estimate that posses have been responsible for some 5,500 murders between 1984-93. Murders by city on an annual basis range from 300 in New York City to 25-30 in Dallas, Texas, to 10 per year in Cleveland, Ohio (International Association Chiefs of Police, 1995).

Firearms Distribution

Jamaican posses gather firearms in a variety of methods common to U.S. street gangs. The purchase of stolen weapons accounts for the greatest number of guns held by the organizations; however, this is not their preferred source. Weapon reliability is of prime concern, therefore major burglaries and robberies of sporting goods stores are a major source of firearms. Posses also pay persons legally authorized to purchase weapons to buy in quantity for them in return for illegal drugs, cash, or both. That posses are far-reaching is best illustrated in that ATF Agents have traced firearms seized from posse members to their purchase only days earlier and half way across the nation (ATF Press Release, Toronto, 1995).

Note: Much information contained in Section I, unless otherwise noted, was gained as a result of "off-the-record" conversations with a variety of law enforcement officials.

SECTION II

Research Setting

The community observed is situated in a declining middle-class neighborhood in a large Midwestern city. The Jamaican Posse crack house is situated in a multi-unit apartment building on a narrow tree-lined street. The surrounding one-half square-mile area is residential in nature and covered with countless apartment units, most of which are built around courtyards. The community is racially mixed.

Four blocks to the north is Main Street; a place marked by rundown bars, countless package goods liquor stores, fast-food stores, and cleaners—a place where immediate gratification sells. It is also there that a low-level, racially integrated street gang sells crack on the public way.

Upon my first visit to this community, my recovering friend and I walked past the building he had earlier identified as the posse crack house. As we passed, a fellow wearing dreadlocks looked up from the sedan he was waxing, asking if we wanted to get "messed up." My companion laughed, stating that he was in recovery. The Jamaican then turned to me. "How about you, man? We got the best deals in town," he said.

I asked him how he could be so sure that I was not a policeman. He threw back his head in laughter. "I'm a respectable man and so are all of my friends inside that building," he said, indicating toward the crack house. "If you were the police, you would be up on Main Street rousting those little gang-bangers." Before our research was half over, I came to realize that he was absolutely correct in what he said.

Observations

The front window of the recovery home where my friend lived afforded a clear view of the activity in and out of the posse crack house. Each observation was two hours in duration and ranged from as early as 10 a.m. to as late as 4 a.m.

Parking is difficult within the area observed; and therefore, I was waiting for a motorist to drive off on my second visit to observe when the fellow with the dreadlocks crossed the street in front of me, moving toward the crack house. He then called after a worn out looking woman who turned onto the path toward the building. He called after her that if she was there to buy, to go to the first floor today; but if she was going to the crack house, it had been moved to the third floor. This bit of information proved to be important in that it was now known that two separate groups of buyers/users would be entering the building; some would buy and leave immediately, while others would be spending considerable time therein, getting high in the crack house.

The Crack House Observed

Five observation periods of two hours each were undertaken. The chart on the next page details activity. Since the building is residential, it is impossible to determine what number of those persons who entered the building and remained within were not customers of the crack house.

Chart 1 Time of Day	Persons Entering and Leaving Within 5 Minutes	Persons Entering and Remaining Within
10 a.m. – Noon	34	12
3 p.m. – 5 p.m.	29	17
6 p.m. – 8 p.m.	43	20
11 p.m. – 1 a.m.	35	8
1 a.m. – 3 a.m.	22	9
2 a.m. – 4 a.m.	37	6

Police Coverage

Uniformed patrol cars passed the crack house once, once, 3 times, 3 times, 4 times, and twice in keeping with the top-to-bottom times of the above chart. On four such occasions people were on their way into the crack house, and twice persons who had entered only moments before were seen leaving the building as the police passed by. At no time during the observation did any form of proactive policing occur, and accordingly no arrests were made. On one occasion, during the 6 p.m. – 8 p.m. observation, the same fellow I encountered in front of the crack house was exiting his sedan when a patrol car passed by. He waved and smiled toward its female driver who nodded his way and drove off. At no time were any apparent specialized police units noted in the area observed.

Comparative Observation

A series of five two-hour observations of the street gang on Main Street was also undertaken making use of the seclusion of a mini-van. Typically between seven and ten gang members were present on a particular street corner. Their behaviors were marked by strutting about, loud talk designed to call attention to themselves, and verbal and non-verbal communications apparently designed to intimidate those passing by.

They also sold crack on the street. Buyers would approach the group and after a brief conversation one of them would walk some thirty feet away to where a paper bag rested in the doorway of a boarded-up storefront. The gang member would take the crack from the bag, return to the corner where he and the buyer would shake hands and exchange the bag for money.

During the five periods of observation between two and five sales occurred on each occasion. It is to be noted that gang observations were not conducted at like time periods as those of the posse crack house and therefore comparative analyses become invalid.

The Main Street gang members attracted far greater police attention than did the Jamaican Posse crack house. Police passed by an average of seven times per two-hour observation period, conducted field interrogations on six occasions, and made arrests twice; however, neither arrest was for the sale of drugs, nor was the "stashed" drug bag confiscated.

Talking to the Police

As a former police officer, it is likely that I am considered by some as at least an associate member of the police subculture. I was therefore able to arrange conversations with six officers who are regularly assigned to the observed area (the posse crack house and Main Street are both on the same police beat). In each instance the officers were asked the following questions, always in the order presented below:

Who is responsible for the sale of crack on your beat? And: Are there members of the Jamaican Posse nearby?

As to the first question, five of six patrol officers said that whatever crack was being sold was the work of the Main Street gang members. The other officer said she was unaware of crack sales on her beat.

As to the presence of the Jamaican Posse, all six stated that they were unaware of the posse's presence in the area. Three did comment that they were of the opinion that the posse does operate in the next city over (the observed area is beside the city limits). Two others said that they had once arrested Jamaicans for Unlawful Use of Weapons, but they had no idea as to whether they were posse members.

Former Crack Users Interviewed

None of the men living in the halfway house where my recovering friend lived had used drugs in that community; however, I was put in touch with other members of the recovering community who had. Six women and five men were interviewed. All had been in recovery for less than six months' time, so all had "copped" crack in the area observed within the past six months. Each was asked two questions:
Who is the major supplier of crack in that community? And: Who did you buy from?

All eleven recovering addicts stated without hesitation that crack was 98% under the control of the Jamaican Posse. Similarly, each mentioned the crack house in question.

As to their most frequent source of the drug, all but one male said that they bought from the Jamaican Posse. The other explained that his cousin had been killed by the posse in New York and therefore, he avoided them.

One woman noted that occasionally she would buy from the Main Street gang members for convenience sake, if she was getting off a bus on their street corner, but otherwise not. She voiced concern over the undue attention the gang places on themselves by what she termed "jive-ass behavior."

Other noteworthy comments were made by certain of the recovering addicts. A woman explained that she had been a frequent visitor of the posse crack house and that over the period of a year the crack house itself (where buyers smoked the drug) was moved between one apartment and another, sometimes as often as twice weekly. Similarly, she and several others stated that the sales apartment was likewise moved about within the building on an almost weekly basis.

One veteran of over ten years of crack addiction recounted the time when the posse first moved into the community. He recalled two issues of significance: First, that the posse was able to seize control of sales of the drug from earlier members of the Main Street gang members simply by announcing their arrival. The posse's well-known reputation for extreme violence and their vastly superior numbers were sufficient to convince the gang members that they had no option but to submit to the newcomers.

Second, of perhaps greater interest is the manner in which the posse came upon the observed community. It seems that shortly after the arrival of crack in the city in question, a wonderful little Jamaican restaurant opened—and still exists—less than two blocks away from what is now the posse crack house. Posse members patronizing the restaurant evaluated the market for crack, and probably the relative weakness of the Main Street gang members, and apparently said, "Why not . . . ?"

The same person also told of an incident several years ago in which several posse members shot and wounded a police officer in a shootout during a foiled robbery attempt. Though the would-be robbers were members of a different posse, word arrived at the posse crack house (where our information source was present) within an hour of the incident. An hour later the entire operation was shut down and the building emptied. Two weeks later, the source recalls, the crack operation was re-opened with an entirely new posse staff.

SECTION III

Section III centers upon several aspects of the Jamaican Posses, namely:

1. Their ability to conquer drug trade by a willingness to act out extreme violence.
2. Their superior numbers which enable them to recruit additional members on short notice.
3. The fact that posse ranking members and middle-echelon parties maintain a low profile.
4. Posse organization is loose and informal in nature.
5. Posse splinter groups have set up drug trade in new cities in an almost casual fashion.

Each of these issues will be treated as they apply to the observed Jamaican Posse crack operation.

Use of Violence

The word of our information source seems credible as to the silent takeover of the posse from the Main Street gang members. Review of a 1984 police intelligence document indicates that the gang had some 25 active members. Even if they were inclined to confront the posse in violence (which is doubtful), the posse could have easily produced ten times that number of Jamaicans on a moment's notice. Clearly the gang did the smart thing in relinquishing control of crack sales to the posse as they did.

The Posse's Low Profile

Police develop a system of visual shorthand categorization, a process Jerome Skolnick (1966) refers to as the symbolic assailant. The basis for this process is the logic that if one stands on a gang's street corner and dresses as do those gang members, he too is probably a gang member.

At the inception of the infamous Blackstone Rangers in Chicago, Jeff Fort and his underlings were in the business of fighting the rival Black Disciples and so it is not surprising that they engaged in strutting and intimidating street-corner behaviors designed to call attention to themselves. However, within five years' time (1969) Fort's organization had grown to 7,000 members and had evolved into the Black P Stone Nation (Pincomb & Seibel, 1994). By then Fort obviously realized that his future rested in organized crime, for he and other members of his Main 21 ruling body would never be seen engaging in behaviors likely to attract police attention. To the contrary, the only time the police would see Fort or his people was during brief stops on 47th Street to give workers instructions.

Jamaican Posse members do not engage in street-corner behaviors which are counter productive to their goals and objectives. Nor do they fit the image of common police perceptions of what gangsters or drug dealers are supposed to look like. To the contrary, Jamaicans in general assimilate well into middle-class respectability. They speak English beautifully and usually without street idioms. Posse members dress well and drive expensive autos (as did the member encountered in front of the crack house); however, the clothes are more fashionable than flashy, and the cars are anything but the stereotypical "pimp mobile" favored by many U.S. drug dealers and gang leaders.

The literature is rich with materials dealing with the differing ways that police deal with the public. The powerless are invariably subject to more proactive policing than are the powerful, or those who might be powerful (Westley, 1970). Police develop a shorthand means of categorizing groups of people, ranging from those who are used to being stopped by the police to those who are most likely to become indignant at being questioned.

In this case, the relative settings doubtless play a part in police decisions as to whether or not to stop and question either people in and out of the Jamaican Posse crack house and also the Main Street gang members. In the first case, the crack house is centered within a residential area and is not subject to use as a "living room" for street persons. As a result, the police are unlikely to categorize people on foot in that area as members of the street subculture. Additionally, during the course of the observation, numerous people were witnessed carrying briefcases and other items indicating their employed status. More significantly, very few persons apparently connected with the crack house operation were observed at all; and those who were moved directly between their autos and the building and were therefore potential police targets for only brief seconds.

The above comments, however, fail to explain the safe passage of the crack house clientele in that almost all of those parties certainly did fit the model of street types copping drugs. One possible explanation for police inattention toward them might rest in the fact that the physical geography of the area acts against keen police observation. The narrow tree-lined streets make it quite difficult to view pedestrians from a distance. Or perhaps the police are simply satisfied that they already know where the crack traffic is (on Main Street) and that they are simply not attuned to seeking suspicious behavior in that area. By contrast the Main Street gang members might as well wear gang colors with "symbolic assailant" written across their chests. Recall the comment of one recovering addict calling them "jive-asses." All of their behaviors are unsophisticated, act against successful drug dealing, and are designed simply to say **look at us**. Is it any wonder that the posse apparently allows them their little nearby dealing corner considering the remarkable amount of "heat" they place on themselves, and consequently take off the posse crack house?

The Informal Nature of Posse Organization

In those areas where "crime is normal" actors gain status within the community in precisely the same manner as to fine athletes and outstanding students in other places (LeFlore, 1982). Within this framework it is often seemingly more important for gang leaders and drug dealers to be known and celebrated than to reap the rewards of criminal success. Such persons know full well that their high profile places their illegal operations in jeopardy, yet most take the attitude that the money is without value unless they are known for what they accomplish.

The legend of Don Juan Williams illustrates this point well. For nearly two decades Williams controlled the majority of the cocaine dispensed on the West Side of

Chicago, a fact he celebrated by dying his hair green and gold. He kept a stable of classic autos all in the same color scheme, and one of his favorite outfits was a green sequined jumpsuit with huge dollar signs across the front and back. In season he could be seen in his box directly behind the Chicago Bulls bench. Though he survived parading around the inner city as he did for many years, once he began "high-fiving" NBA stars, the federal government took an active interest in his activities and thus his downfall.

The success of this Jamaican Posse crack operation rests in the fact that no person or group of persons made their business known, not even to those within the drug subculture. Though the group of recovering addicts was not specifically asked the identity of posse leaders, the issue did arise in several conversations. None of those interviewed knew anything about the organization save the account as to a complete turnover of staff immediately following the police shooting.

One possible explanation for posse leaders staying quietly out of sight is the fact that they are from another land and therefore have both different values and needs than their American counterparts. Or perhaps they are simply brighter criminals. In either case they have avoided being the targets of the police, something which all criminal celebrities become.

I recall immediately after graduating from the police academy and being assigned to the

Prairie Avenue District, deciding that my primary goal was to be winning the cat-and-mouse game with Jeff Fort and the Black P Stone Nation. By comparison, a police recruit today might be assigned to the area where the Jamaican Posse apparently sells millions of dollars of cocaine; and he/she would not only know nothing about the operation or its leaders, but he/she would not have anyone else capable of telling him/her either.

Formation of Posse Splinter Groups

As treated earlier in this text, it appears that the observed posse crack house came about simply because certain members traveled to that area in order to dine on Jamaican food. However, it is significant that their resulting success was not simply the result of a whim, but rather due to their well developed reputation for violence. Clearly, this operation opened in much the same manner as those in cities where posse members initially visited while on vacation.

Conclusion

The Jamaican Posse observed is situated in a densely populated residential area where constant pedestrian traffic in and out of their crack house apparently does not attract the attention of either neighboring residents or the local police. Their criminal organization is totally internal in nature in that all sales and drug use occurs within the confines of their own apartment building.

The posse is notable for their resistance to unsophisticated ego-inflating behaviors that are commonly associated with street gang members who deal drugs. That the posse observed is under highly intelligent leadership is evidenced by their constant switching of spaces within the building—an act clearly designed to circumvent the potential of law enforcement gaining warrants to search their premises. By the time the police might outline illegal activities in one certain unit, the activities are moved elsewhere.

The manner in which the posse shut down all activities immediately following the shooting of a police officer, and its subsequent reopening under an entirely different staff, indicates both thoughtful decision making and a large and flexible organization, much in keeping with the literature.

Clearly absent from the observed setting are the guns and terror often associated with the posses. However, within the context of their rich history of overpowering weak drug organizations, it becomes clear that their only reasons for not resorting to violence was the total surrender of the Main Street gang members. Finally, that the posse opened their crack house simply because they visited a nearby restaurant substantiates the literature as to their operating on whims as they move into new territories.

Notes

Jamaican Posse criminal activities are not limited to the illegal sale of drugs, a point illustrated by the robbery attempt of a Chicago currency exchange of February 15, 1992, by members of the Dunkirk Posse (as noted previously). A month later in Bayshore, New York, four masked members of the Dunkirk Posse ambushed two check-cashing workers, killing a retired New York City police officer.

Recently in a Chicago suburb a posse member obtained credit reports on 1,000 persons through an authorized information source while posing as a real estate investor. Subsequent investigation of the first 50 persons whose credit data had been gained disclosed illegal credits to charge accounts of over $300.000. The investigation continues.

Such diversity clearly aligns the Jamaican Posse with white organized crime of past generations and warns observers that they are far more than simply street thugs with guns.

This and other research on Jamaican Posses begs the question as to how a criminal organization of such far-reaching magnitude could remain totally anonymous to all but the most enlightened law enforcement officials. Two theories are prominent. The first rests in the media's reluctance over the past decade to name street gangs. However, many sensational exceptions to that policy have occurred. Perhaps the notion of one federal law enforcement agent who contributed information to this work may have the actual solution to this mystery. It is his opinion that the media hushes posse crime in deference to airlines and the travel industry who fear negative tourist reaction to accounts of treachery committed by persons from tropical places.

ARTICLE 22 — *Drug Cultures Expand Beyond Major City Limits*

In a nearby suburb of a major city the police were out in full force on a bright spring afternoon. An officer riding a bike made his way back and forth looking inside vehicles backed up to a stop sign, seeking seatbelt violators. Each was issued a non-traffic violation carrying a $20 fine. It was a good reminder of the importance of safety measures, generated a good bit of extra revenue for the town, and kept a half-dozen officers busy in the process.

This is not to say that there was no downside to the seatbelt roadblock, however, in that at the very moment all of this was going on there were a trio of street-walking prostitutes plying their trade on a nearby main street notable for its transient motels. If one looked carefully, it was also possible to see at least one pimp standing across the street from where the women were busy waving at passing motorists.

Thus the question becomes whether this village of tree-lined streets is the quiet, crime-free place it seems at first glance, or is it something quite different from that? Ask the guy behind the counter of a snack shop situated directly between two dive motels: "I'll have a cop in line waiting for a sandwich next to a housewife with her kids, and behind them will be a crack head hooker with her eyes popping out of her head looking around for something to steal. I just try getting them in and out of here as fast as I can. As for the hookers, a lot of the people here don't even know that this prostitution is going on."

Ask a cab driver who works overnights in town about what really goes on as to crime and drug use. "I stop in the gas station a block away from those motels and at 3 a.m. there's a half-dozen crack dealers selling and negotiating, either inside the station or outside on the driveway. Hookers in and out turning their cash over to their pimps, and the cops have no clue. Some think they don't care about the drug culture being here, but I don't think they even know what's going on in front of their noses. They got hired to be cops in a quiet place, and that's all they're good for."

Another cab driver from the next town over told about how the prostitutes and drug dealers work out of the transient motels. "In (the next town over) the dive motels cost a little less but the junkies don't use them anymore because the cops there are street-smart and know what time it is. They hit the place with search warrants, so they call me and I drop them over here.

"There are so many crack heads in those two (motels) that the management doesn't even take straight people anymore. They tell us not to bring them any kind of straight tourists, because they're afraid a decent person will call about all the drug activity in and out of the places."

So if cab drivers and restaurant workers, and anyone with eyes, all know exactly what is going on, what about the police? One theory might be that they have never been around street criminals and therefore do not recognize their behaviors as being associated with crime. Another theory is that the police have a policy that as long as everything looks fine to the average resident, the best police plan is to do nothing.

Two Nights of Observation

Over the course of an early-summer weekend two lone male researchers observed the three-block stretch in question for five hours, from 11 p.m. to 4 a.m. Observations follow:

11 p.m. – Midnight

Two women, one white, the other Black were "working the street," waving at passing motorists, jumping in and out of autos. The dates were not followed after having picked the women up, therefore it is not known where the acts in question were carried out. Two vehicles pulled into the lot of one of the two motels. One truck contained four individuals who appeared to be college age. A white male came out from a motel room, reached into the truck, which then immediately drove off. Later, two high school age youths entered the same lot, the same man came outside. The driver met him in the parking lot, and the two shook hands, apparently exchanging money for drugs.

Midnight – 1 a.m.

The two women observed above were both in the all-night gas station buying energy drinks. One was telling the other in a tone which could be heard from twenty feet away that her last date had really gotten rough with her, and wanted more time with her but was not willing to pay for it. The white woman was later seen waving at passing autos. A car full of drunks entered the other motel lot and talked to a Black male who was talking on a public phone at the mouth of the entrance. He told the drunks to shut up and stop attracting attention before they got him in trouble. He then went over to the car and reached inside. The car then drove off.

1 a.m. – 2 a.m.

The Black woman was now in and out of two autos within a twenty-minute segment. During the same time a car full of rowdy youths pulled to the curb and began mocking the white hooker. This resulted in the appearance of her apparent pimp who reached toward his waistband as if to draw a firearm. The car sped away and the woman and her protector walked to one of the motels and went inside.

2 a.m. – 3 a.m.

Certain nearby bars just closed as there was a great deal of vehicular traffic and loud noises coming from within. Two such cars pulled into the motel where the pay phone was, and a pair of Black men told them to quiet down or get away, as their behavior was going to "front him off" with the police. It is not known whether or not they bought drugs while at the motel.

3 a.m. – 4 a.m.

The street quieted down. A cab driver with a passenger inside pulled into the gas station and made a call from his cell phone. A white man appeared on foot a moment later, got inside the rear sear with the passenger, then left seconds later. The white woman was once again on the street waving at passing vehicles.

4 a.m. – 5 a.m.

Both the woman and the man who had earlier scared off the car full of drunks walked several blocks to the east and had breakfast at an all-night diner. No activity was noted at the motels.

It is to be noted that over the five hours of observation an average of one squad car drove by perhaps each half-hour. None slowed upon nearing the motels, and none stopped to talk to either of the women who continuously waved at passing motorists. Nor did the police become curious enough to stop and ask the researchers the nature of their business, having been continuously on the street in the same pair of cars for a five-hour period. Whether disinterested or oblivious to crime conditions, what is certain is that the police were not acting upon either curiosity or suspicion that typically drives effective police officers.

————————————

Intelligent criminals give thought to decisions as to where they will carry out their illegal acts. Much of that decision-making has to do with their evaluation of the police. Different departments may have quite diverse priorities. Where the chief of key administrators comes from a background in the traffic division, they may pass that interest along to their officers. By contrast, if the decision-makers come from "street cop" backgrounds, then it is likely that their department will lean heavily toward proactive policing, aggressive tactical teams, and large investigative divisions.

Suppose that in Department A administrators emphasize seatbelt violations and writing a large number of moving traffic violations. In the next town the chief had been a narcotics commander and therefore emphasizes a proactive search for those possessing and dealing drugs. Word on the street will move within the drug community that it is difficult to walk a block down the street without being stopped and questioned in what seems like never-ending field interrogations. Informal discussions among members of the drug culture will soon result in their moving their dealing activities to the nearby town where officers commonly drive past crack dealers in search of seatbelt violations. By making such changes drug users and dealers can significantly reduce the probability that they will be arrested.

Individuals do not normally apply to a great many different departments during their job search. Rather, applicants are likely to speak to their college instructors seeking information about a variety of police agencies. They also commonly speak to working officers to learn what their work experience is with their department. As a result of this inquiry process, most police applicants have a good idea about department priorities and style, crime conditions, and officer attitudes.

Thus at the time of making application to a certain police department, most hopeful recruits pretty much know what would be expected of them if they were to be hired by a certain agency. Thus, most officers wishing to become primarily crime-fighters apply to major city departments with an active inner-city crime element. By contrast, those wishing to engage in community services, write traffic tickets, and experience a relatively calm police experience are likely to gravitate toward quiet suburban or rural departments.

Herein lies the problem when an inner-city street crime and drug culture moves their center of activities to what was previously a quiet community. The very same officers who had chosen a department for its quiet characteristics suddenly find themselves in the very center of criminal activity and violence. It becomes unfortunate that such officers are likely to be uncomfortable within this type of active crime setting. The problem becomes all the worse by virtue of the fact that veteran officers of the formerly quiet department have no frame of reference as to how to go about confronting street-wise, dangerous criminals. Such veteran officers then do not have the ability to assist the newer officers. Thus, the sudden presence of street crime and violence tends to overwhelm a group of officers who never asked to be called upon to regularly confront dangerous offenders.

ARTICLE 23 — *Inner-City Victimization*

Overview

Numerous victimization studies have concluded much of the following:

1) Not all classes report crimes with the same frequency.
2) Lower-class individuals are less likely to contact the police than members of other classes.
3) White people are more frequent reporters than other racial groups.
4) Both African-Americans and Hispanics report crimes with essentially equal frequency, and at a rate far lower than whites.
5) Most studies indicate that slightly less than 50% of all crime is reported to the police.

The author conducted a simplistic research project in order to learn the present level of cooperation existing between the police and inner-city residents in one major city. For this purpose having been victimized and then making a prompt police report is taken as being indicative of cooperation with authorities.

Sample

One hundred residents of a high-crime-rate inner-city community were asked the following:

1) Have you or anyone in your immediate family been the victim of a serious crime in the past year?

The crimes considered are (a) battery, (b) robbery, (c) sex offense, (d) auto theft, (e) other

2) If so, did you or the victim report the crime to the police?

3) If not, tell why you did not make a police report.

Check one of the following if the crime was not reported.

(a) Lack of confidence in the police.

(b) Lack of confidence in the court system.

(c) Fear of retaliation.

(d) Will handle situation myself.

All of those questioned were African-American individuals residing in a community where the vast majority of residents are public aid recipients. All resided in low-income housing, comprising of one- and two-story row houses.

Findings

Eighty-two of 100 residents stated that they, or someone in their immediate family, had been the victim of a serious offense within the past year's time.

Research Findings

An astounding eighty-two of 100 respondents stated that someone in their immediate household had been the victim of a serious criminal offense. When asked whether or not the crime had been reported to the police, eighteen individuals stated that they had informed the police about the offense, while the remaining sixty-four said that they did not elect to make a police report. The breakdown by crime follows:

Battery

A total of thirty individuals questioned in the survey reported having been battery victims, and only five victims made police reports. Battery is generally described as suffering an injury as the result of being physically attacked. Police reporting procedures break down the offense according to the severity of the attack. Minor injuries are labeled as battery, while attacks causing major injury are aggravated batteries. Since police reports were in no way involved with this research, each battery victim was asked whether or not they were hospitalized. Fourteen of the thirty batteries did result in hospitalization of the victim.

While five of thirty battery victims reported the incidents to the police, a mere two of fourteen victims of aggravated battery made police reports. Thus there appears to be no distinction made by battery victims in terms of their decision regarding whether or not to contact the police based on the severity of injuries suffered.

Of the twenty-five battery victims who did not make police reports, twenty listed their reason for non-reporting as being an intention to even the score through revenge or "street justice." The other five victims of batteries said that they did not have faith in the police to act on their behalf.

Robbery

Robbery is defined as taking property from another by use or threat of force. Armed robbery is accomplished by use of a dangerous weapon. For the purpose of this research no distinction was made as to whether or not a weapon was used in the robbery act. None of the robbery victims were injured seriously in the course of the crimes. Only one victim received as much as a bruised lip.

In all there were thirty-one robbery victims, and only four chose to make a police report. Of the twenty-seven individuals who made no report, twenty-two stated that they intended to handle the matter in their own way: vengeance, retribution, street justice. Four others said that they lacked confidence in the police, while one other victim stated that he did not trust the courts.

That twenty-two of thirty-one robbery victims said that they would get even in their own way is extremely telling in the sense that those individuals apparently had no fear of criminal offenders who made use of violent means to carry out their crimes. Thus, the question is raised as to whether use of violence in the inner city is so normal a function that today's victim may often become tomorrow's offender.

It is notable that one of the choices in responding to victims' reasons for not reporting the incident to the police was fear of retribution; however, not a single victim of battery or robbery apparently was particularly afraid of meeting the offender on a subsequent occasion.

Sex Offenses

A total of ten individuals stated that they had been victims of a sexual attack. The specific nature of the act was not requested, thus no distinction is made between what might have been a forcible rape, or perhaps having been fondled by the offender. Four of those victims did report the incidents to the police; the remaining six victims did not.

When asked for their reasons not to contact the police, five of the six victims said that they lacked faith in the court system, while the one remaining victim stated that he/she did fear retaliation at the hands of the offender. The frequency with which the sex victims stated they lacked faith in the courts might well be taken as a strong indictment against the great leeway defense attorneys have often enjoyed in their attacks upon sex crime victims at trial; tactics where defense cross-examination is designed to place responsibility on the victim for the act. Many victims of sex offenses have stated that their court ordeal was just as terrifying to them as the actual crime against them.

Auto Theft

There were four victims of auto theft accounted for in the research and all of them reported their loss to the police. This condition is in keeping with other victimization reports where auto theft is nearly always reported to the police. This is not surprising because auto theft victims must enlist the police in their search if they hope to have their car restored to them. Similarly, insurance companies routinely expect that the victim will make a report to the police.

Seven other unspecified offenses were included in the research, and only one such victim did make a police report.

Research Summary

That eighty-two percent of the households surveyed had experienced victimization within the preceding year indicates that inner-city crime might be at least twice as great as otherwise imagined. When one considers the impact on both the police and courts were all crime victims to make police reports, authorities would be faced with investigating more than four times more serious criminal incidents that they currently receive. To the extent that the police clearance rate remained somewhat constant, criminal courts would also have quadruple the number of defendants entering the system. Thus the need for many more judges, prosecutors, public defenders, and all other court personnel.

From a societal point of view this research tends to strongly support that inner-city residents do in fact see crime as a quite normal function of their society. When one is victimized, more often than not they do not use the police or courts, which seem to be seen as officials for others away from their own lower-class community. When it comes to such violent acts as battery and robbery, members of that community seem most willing to deal with the issue in their own manner, which seemingly would call for more violence on their own part. To the extent that this is true and correct, one might also make the statement that violence is seen as a tool to be used in a routine manner when called for within many inner-city settings.

Most criminals are very much like other workers in the sense that they wish for their job to go as smoothly as possible. In the case of the robber that means that they must gain control of the interaction with their victim, get him to do as told, gain the sought-after property, and make good their getaway without incident.

Control of the victim is typically gained either through the display of a dangerous weapon, or by threatening the use of force. Robbery offenders then give orders as to what is expected of the victim. Property is then either turned over to the offender or taken from the victim. The offender then flees from the crime scene in order to best disassociate himself from the crime.

When robbery offenses go this smoothly, the offender's chances of escaping arrest are great. In the first place the robber's chances of initially getting away without being apprehended by the police are good. Secondly, when the offense occurs without the victim being injured in the course of the act, the robber's chances of escaping arrest at a later date improve.

Major city investigators have a constant case load, that is to say that new investigative assignments may be nearly a daily event. For that reason investigators have very limited time to spend on any given case. Therefore major cases where a victim is seriously injured takes great precedent over more routine robberies where the victim escapes injury.

Smart criminals are fully aware of the fact that to injure a victim greatly increases the resulting investigative effort. In the words of the street, to seriously injure a robbery victim is to bring about great increased "heat" from the police.

Robber Qualifications

In order for a robber to gain any level of success, a robber must be willing to do the following:

1) Carry a firearm or other dangerous weapon.
2) Use the weapon if called upon to do so.
3) Otherwise exact injury upon a resistant victim.
4) Run the risk of meeting an armed intended victim.
5) Risk discovery by the police while in the act of the crime.

That not all criminals are adept at career planning can be taken from the following case study.

Case Study

Police on patrol nearby a senior citizens' complex witnessed an elderly hunched-over lady repeated whacking an individual prone on the ground with her shopping cart. As police rushed to intervene, they saw a large automatic pistol resting next to the fellow being beaten. Subsequent investigation disclosed that the fellow being pummeled was a very large ex-convict with a record of non-violent offenses. On this occasion he decided to move up the criminal scale and rob the elderly lady at gunpoint. However, when he pointed the weapon at her and announced a robbery, the little old lady was unimpressed. Rather than turn over her purse, she simply began swinging the shopping cart at the offender, knocking him to the ground.

What is significant about this case is that the robber was ill-suited for his work in that most individuals armed with a firearm would have used it on a resisting victim. Fortunately for the old lady this particular robber simply did not have it in him to hurt her.

Unusual Behavior

Most robbers do not wish to complicate their work by injuring their victim. However, most will use force against their victims in those instances where the need to do so seems great. Then there is the small category of robbers as depicted in the case study, who simply lack the violent nature to injure their victim, even while under attack themselves.

A third category of robbers is the sadistic robber as in the following case study.

Case Study

A group of college students went out for a night on the town to celebrate the end of the summer. After having far too much to drink they were approached by two street people who asked them if they wanted to be with a woman. Two agreed to go with them to a nearby housing project. Once within the apartment complex, the two offenders drew guns, announced a robbery, and took the victims' valuables without incident. One of the gunmen then turned as if to walk away, then smiled, and shot both victims point blank in the head, despite the fact that there had been no resistance whatever. The victims were shot simply for the job of committing the act.

An intense police investigation resulted based upon the violent and senseless nature of the crime. Both offenders were sentenced to death. Had they simply walked away without having harmed the robbery victims, chances are excellent that the robbery would have been treated in a more routine manner, and the offenders might never have been arrested at all.

This assessment of the behavior of robbery offenders strongly indicates that by far the best ploy for victims of stick-ups is to follow directions to the letter and hope that they have not run across one of the few sadistic robbers described in the second case study.

ARTICLE 25 — *Police-Criminal Relations*

Overview

Not very smart members of the criminal community may speak poorly or act out negatively toward the police. Within their own limited frame of reference they may believe that they are gaining status from onlookers. However, this type of senseless disrespect toward the police is generally frowned upon based on the belief of most criminals that it is simply not bright to go out of their way to give the police a difficult time.

Case Study

A team of violent crimes investigators were working on a double-homicide. In the course of their work they approached an individual on a street corner who resembled the description of the killer. The investigators got out of their car and called to the suspect who immediately joined the investigators without protest. At the same time another person who had been standing and talking to the suspect began screaming at the investigators as they attempted to question the suspect. After several minutes of continued loud verbal assault upon the police, the suspect himself told his loud friend to shut up. Soon the investigators eliminated the suspect as having been involved in their case. As they thanked the suspect for his cooperation, they did ask the name of the fellow who had caused them so much aggravation.

Soon after the investigators ran the name they had been given of the big-mouthed agitator, they learned that he had an extensive record for armed robberies. From that day on each time they investigated a robbery incident in that area, they included his mugshot among those shown to victims. Soon the fellow was identified for his part in a home invasion robbery, and the police recovered the weapons and the loot from the robbery in the offender's auto. He was found guilty and sentenced to twenty years in prison.

The practical application of that case was that the individual actually was sentenced to prison for having been a jerk to the police investigators. Had he kept his mouth shut when police approached his friend, he never would have come to the initial attention of the police. Therefore, chances are remote that he would have been caught for the subsequent home invasion, at least not by that means.

Case Study

A man with an extensive criminal history was gunned down on the street. The case initially went unsolved until a hand-picked investigator was brought in to take over the case. Police quickly found a woman who knew about the crime as she was associated with the drug organization responsible for the crime. As the investigation progressed, the informant told the police that the offenders had decided to kill the new investigator in the belief that if he were out of the way, they would not be charged.

Not long after, it was determined that individuals thought to be involved with the drug organization attempted to follow the investigator as he left police headquarters to go to his home. Once authorities learned of this, a task force was immediately formed involving more than fifty investigators. Soon, the three gunmen responsible for the killing were arrested and charged. Then the drug aspect of the investigation was taken up by the task force. The result was that more than twenty members of the criminal organization were charged with a 100-count indictment based on a variety of possessions with intent to deliver controlled substances.

Both of the above case studies illustrate that the police have a great deal of discretion in terms of how they conduct investigations and that the scope of such investigations is likely to enlarge significantly when it appears that members of the criminal community wish to place the police at risk. In such instances the police subculture tends to close ranks and look out for one another.

Intelligent criminals well understand that the real live game of cops and robbers is a challenge for offenders to win without their creating personal situations with the police. It is important to understand that many members of the criminal community are involved in one type of crime or another on virtually a daily basis. Should the criminal needlessly antagonize a given officer, it is often possible for them to spend every free moment investigating the behavior of the targeted individual. In that manner the police might literally shut down a criminal's ability to function as they wish.

Use of Non-Traditional Police Tactics

The Problem

A middle-class guy from the suburbs got shotgunned to death in an alley on the West Side of Chicago. Experience told my partner and me that he was there either to buy drugs or to visit a street-walking prostitute.

When such crimes take place in the inner-city, street criminals act in front of one another and they freely discuss their acts with one another. For these reasons we knew full well that the stick-ups, addicts, pimps, and whores presently on the street knew exactly who had committed the crime. How to find out was the problem.

The Scene Before Us

It was late morning on a bright and sunny day as we drove westbound on Madison Street, trying our best not to run over the empty beer and wine bottles and old needles and syringes discarded during the overnight of street activity. A tiny hooker known as "Little Bit" was waving at passing motorists as we approached, and her pimp, "Frankie the Wonder Boy," stood across the street close by to protect her as need be. My partner Foley and I knew without question that the pair knew exactly who had killed our victim and why.

Choices

1) We could arrest her as a loitering prostitute and take her to the station and use the arrest as leverage to induce her to talk about the murder.
2) We could threaten both of them with the prospect of arrest and then ask for the same information.
3) Or we could gather the pair and simply ask them who did it.

Weighing the Options

Police are often successful in playing "Let's Make a Deal" with street criminals. The idea is: You tell me what you know and I either don't charge you after all or I help you in court in return for the information. However, in this instance a simple loitering charge would not be strong enough to induce her to talk.

As to the second option, there is an old street saying that goes, "You cannot threaten someone with nothing to lose." That means that hard-core criminals have done time in prison and probably have met violence themselves many times over. So threats seldom are effective.

Instead, we just began a conversation with Little Bit and asked her to motion to Frankie the Wonder Boy to join us. When asked about the murder, they, of course, denied knowledge

185

during which time we noticed the very early signs of heroin withdrawal in both of them. This brings to mind another important street lesson for every young cop. Never, ever trust anything an addict tells you unless you are in a position to severely damage his position by arrest and jail time. The idea is that addicts will tell you anything they think you want to hear just so they don't have to suffer through heroin withdrawal or to keep them from the next rock of crack.

Use of Humor Rather Than Authority

Once we had gone over it with the pair twice, it was clear that they were not going to tell us anything so we left asking if they wanted submarines for lunch. They thought that we were kidding.

An hour later Foley and I returned to the same corner of Madison Street to find Wonder Boy present but Little Bit was off somewhere turning a trick. I was opening the car door when she hopped out of a station wagon driven by someone's husband and dad who looked a bit like Ward Cleaver of the old "Leave it to Beaver" show.

By then Foley had set up a pair of folding chairs and spread a checkered tablecloth over our little cooler. We then handed the hooker and her pimp their sandwiches. The pair stood frozen in front of us as we discarded our suit jackets so that our guns and holsters were now gleaming in the sunlight.

Two bites into my sub and a brown Ford pulled to the curb to negotiate business with

Little Bit; however, Foley smiled and waved and asked the driver how much he was prepared to pay for sex with Little Bit. He turned white as a ghost and sped off never looking back. This scene repeated itself over two dozen times in the next 90 minutes. We had cost the pair about $400 since we began our friendly picnic with them.

All the while we knew that they desperately needed a whole lot of money in a big hurry to feed their respective heroin habits. Most importantly, we were as kind and friendly to them as any picnic host would be expected to be. The two of them simply shook their heads in apparent disbelief that we knew how to kill them with kindness.

Finally, Frankie the Wonder Boy surrendered with an actual smile and tossed a paper to the ground, which I picked up only after being certain that no other street people had seen him drop it. Soon we were packed up and gone.

An hour later we arrested a pimp by the name of Magic Juan Hughes for the murder. The next night we found Nina the Nun, his hooker, who had the shotgun used in the crime in her apartment. Her trick had made the mistake of showing her a large roll of money before she began her sex act with him. Instead, she motioned to Magic by opening and closing the door, which made the dome light go on and off, which was the signal that money awaited them. So Magic shot the father of four as Nina fled the car.

We solved a very nasty crime in a very short period of time without the use of either threats or unkind words to anyone. We simply understood criminal behavior: Little Bit needed to work to feed two heroin habits, and the pair probably actually appreciated that we went about our work in a good-natured and humorous way. And, of course, Frankie had only dropped the bag with the killers' names on it to the ground so that he and Nina might return to work.

For many decades the decision as to felony charging was left in the hands of police criminal investigators. Then in the early-1970s the charging task was given to prosecutors, due primarily to the increasing volume of weak cases sent to felony courts.

The decision to make felony charging a function of the prosecutor's office was designed to allow an objective view of the case facts and strength of evidence. The police-prosecutor process usually involves police investigators to follow leads, gather evidence, and question suspects. A member of the felony review unit is then summoned to the police facility where the prosecutor reviews police reports; interviews the police, witnesses and suspects; then makes a determination as to whether or not felony charges are to be placed against a criminal suspect. When the events occur as generally described herein, the prosecutor has the benefit of objectivity in that he/she was in no way involved in the investigative aspect of the case. By contrast, a police investigator who sees a need to gather evidence against a particular suspect does so with the belief that it is highly possible that such person is, in fact, guilty; otherwise why would they have taken such investigative steps in the first place? Thus, the police investigator may be predisposed to believe in the suspect's guilt.

Task Forces Described

Many major jurisdictions have prosecutors' offices with directors in charge of specialized units such as homicide, gang crimes, organized crimes, and cold case investigations. Under such programs the prosecutor actually has hands-on direction over a specialized group of police investigators.

The notion behind such task force units is that when led by a prosecutor, the police are unlikely to make legal errors which would compromise investigations or taint court cases. It is quite possible that fewer legal errors do occur under such arrangements, however the task force format causes the potential of a far greater problem.

What is Objectivity?

The moment that a prosecutor assumes a law enforcement role, he is functioning as an investigator, plotting strategy to best gather incriminating evidence against a particular targeted suspect.

Case Study

A young woman was found raped and murdered in her suburban apartment. She died of massive blunt trauma wounds to the head and strangulation. She also suffered multiple superficial lacerations to her backside, a bite mark, and several strangely configured puncture wounds at the rear of her waistline.

Soon after the crime, a neighbor of the victim's called police to say that he had experienced a dream on the night of the crime in which a young woman was struck about the head with a blunt object. The police rightly believed that the caller probably made up the dream account out of a need to be caught and punished for the crime.

Police immediately contacted the prosecutor's office, telling them about the alleged dream, and from that moment on every move made by the police was under the direction of the prosecutor.

The case did not go as the police expected in that the alleged dreamer did not confess to the crime as someone wishing to be caught would do. The alleged dream did contain blunt trauma wounds to the head, as in the actual crime. However, the suspect's dream account did not contain any of the other attack aspects the actual victim suffered, including strangulation, bite marks, or mutilation wounds.

Despite their lack of a confession and obvious differences in terms of the other wounds, the suspect was arrested and charged with rape and murder. The suspect was convicted of murder but not rape. The case moved back and forth through the appeal process, then a decade later the state dropped the charges against the suspect only days before a retrial was to occur.

The inherent problem with the state's case was a lack of an objective eye in terms of evaluating the actual weight of evidence present against someone who turned out to be an innocent suspect. To the extent that prosecutors become involved in plotting strategy against a targeted suspect, there ceases to be neutrality within the decision-making process.

ARTICLE 27 — *Victim Participation in Prosecution*

Victimization Revisited

Not all groups of people report crimes equally. Lower-class non-whites report crimes with far less frequency than do others. Many of the same individuals who do not report having been victimized also often refuse to cooperate in prosecutions in those instances where authorities identify guilty parties.

Overview

There are times when the police become aware of crimes without benefit of the victim's assistance. In some instances the police may come upon a crime "on view" as it is occurring. Other times the police are called to a crime scene by a witness not involved in the event. In these and other instances, the police may identify the offender in conjunction with their immediate response to the crime. Many times the result is that the police have actually made an arrest prior to speaking to the victim.

Very often, the same type of individual who would never have called the police to report having been victimized, will respond to the police arrest by stating that they do not wish to sign a complaint against the offender and have no interest in participating in the prosecution process.

Prosecutorial Policies

In many major jurisdictions including Cook County, Illinois (Chicago and suburbs) prosecutors operate on the basis that there will be no felony charges placed unless the victim is willing to sign a criminal complaint binding the accused to the offense, and then follow up by cooperating with the prosecution which includes testifying in court.

The policy not to charge without the support of the victim is based on a belief that if the victim does not care about what was done to him/her, the idea of forcing him/her to appear and testify by use of subpoena is simply not a good one. On many occasions reluctant victims have had a strongly adverse effect upon the trial results. It is not unusual for victims to change their testimony by making statements which might clear the suspect of wrongdoing. Other times they may state under oath that the state forced them to appear in court and testify against their will.

In other jurisdictions felony cases are routinely tried on the basis of having to deal with reluctant victims. The philosophical logic behind that policy is that the prosecutor's responsibility is to society as a whole, and that to rid the community of dangerous felons should be their mission statement. To the extent that a prosecutor's office takes that position, the act of the suspect upon society is the key issue, and whether or not the victim wishes to prosecute is incidental.

Case Study

In Cook County, Illinois, a newspaper reporter received an anonymously mailed film which was alleged to show the performer R. Kelly having sex with an underage girl. The film was turned over to authorities who were satisfied that the adult male was the celebrity. They then embarked on an investigation into the identity of the girl. Investigators eventually took the position that Kelly had committed the acts in question six or seven years earlier and that the girl would have been about age 14 at the time of the incident.

The girl was located and steadfastly denied that she was the girl in the film, and also denied that she had ever been with Kelly under any circumstances. At this juncture in their investigation the authorities were faced with a dilemma. They were very convinced that Kelly was the male subject in the film, as they were able to match furniture and wall hangings in the film background to a room in the suspect's house. At the same time, the prosecutors had to decide whether or not they wanted to violate their own policy of not trying cases without benefit of a cooperating victim.

They did decide to move forward with the prosecution, basing their case primarily on the nature of evidence attached to the film. Additionally, prosecutors made an unusual decision to turn their informant who had identified the alleged girl in the film into their lead courtroom witness. Therefore, the information source who ordinarily never would have even been identified was to be fronted by the state and used to tell just how it happened that she knew the young girl.

As one might imagine, without the testimony of the victim the accused performer was found not guilty of all charges. Thus, this experience may have acted to reinforce their long-standing policy against prosecutions without the benefit of the victim's cooperation.

Case Study

Police on patrol saw a pair of individuals pinning someone up against the side of a building. Police grabbed the men and quickly saw that one offender had a knife to the victim's throat while the other went through his pockets. Officers quickly seized the weapon, the victim's money, and arrested the robbers. They soon learned that the victim was intoxicated to the extent that he was unable to put two words together.

The case then moved to the police station where the victim was fed black coffee; however, with the passing of time, he was no more able to tell the police or anyone else what happened to him. The felony review state's attorney weighed the evidence and decided that the testimony of the officers who were actual witnesses to the offense was not sufficient to place felony armed robbery charges. Without the testimony of the victim there would be no felony charges.

_____

The feeling of the prosecutor was that testimony from the victim was key and essential to a finding of guilty. If the case were to go to trial without the victim's testimony, the state's case would have a hole in it. Further, it would inevitably come out that the victim was highly intoxicated at the time of the offense, another weakness in the prosecution.

In many instances when felony charges are rejected, matching misdemeanor charges will result. For example, in the case of an armed robbery, the offender might be charged with both theft and assault with a weapon, the two included offenses in the armed robbery. In such instances the police officers would testify as to what they saw in the misdemeanor court. Judges are familiar with reduced felony offenses being sent to the lower court, and often hand down maximum sentences as a result.

Case Study

An off-duty police officer was on his way home when he came upon an attack of a young woman, screaming as a large attacker ripped at her clothing. The officer announced his office and began a foot chase that lasted several blocks. The attacker then refused the officer's order to surrender. Several moments went by before police assistance appeared. When finally arrested, the attacker was in possession of a live shotgun shell. He was taken to the station in anticipation of locating the woman he had victimized.

Despite extensive police efforts to locate the victim, she never was located. Therefore the only actual remaining charge against the suspect was for possession of firearm ammunition. He was then sent to misdemeanor court. The arrest report explained the circumstances surrounding the incident, as did the officer's testimony. The result was that the offender received a maximum sentence of one year in jail for a minor weapons violation, which normally would have carried a sentence of probation. Once again the misdemeanor judge understood the significance of the charges before him, and the fact that the actual acts involved were far greater than the formal charges before the court.

ARTICLE 28 — *The Interrogation-Criminal Investigation Connection*

Overview

Over the past half-century a number of instructional books on custodial interrogation have offered poor and sometimes illegal advice to police interrogators. Dating back to the mid-1960s the Miranda Court reviewed these books which they referred to as "police manuals." The nature of the works made suggestions, which included creating fake police line-ups so that suspects would believe that they were identified as offenders. Numerous books suggested that police interrogators must be willing to lie to suspects about the existence of evidence against them, so that the suspects would consider further denials a waste of time. Similarly, one of the primary interrogation manuals suggested that interrogators begin interaction with suspects with a blanket statement that the interrogator knows that the suspect is guilty.

Much of the interrogation literature then and now is also based on the dubious proposition that guilty suspects give off indicators of their guilt through non-verbal behaviors. This concept is most popular with interrogators linked to polygraph testing, which is based essentially on physiological responses to being asked questions about one's actions.

Examination of Written Materials

One of the "police manuals" the Miranda Court reviewed was *Police Interrogation* by Inbau and Reid, first published in 1962. Fred Inbau was a conservative law professor at Northwestern University and John Reid was the founder of a polygraph institute bearing his name. Though the title has changed through several incarnations, a revised version of the early text is still read within police circles.

Consider their statement that police interrogators must be willing to lie to suspects. The context within which this statement is presented deals primarily with stating to suspects that certain forms of evidence links them to the crime when such is actually not the case. Prime examples of such police lies might be that the suspect's bloody fingerprints were lifted from a homicide crime scene. Or that a witness to a street killing has positively identified a photo of the suspect as having been the killer.

The risks to such dishonest and illegal statements on the part of the police are great. If the suspect does believe the lie he/she is being told, he/she might assume that he/she already has one foot on death row. So when the interrogator states that the suspect had better confess to the offense in order to escape the death penalty, the statement might be taken as being true. Thus, the chances of an innocent suspect making a false confession becomes a very real possibility.

The other Inbau and Reid suggestion of starting conversations with suspects with the assurance of their guilt is bad advice on two different levels. If an innocent suspect is informed that the interrogator is already certain of his/her guilt, the suspect is likely to feel that his/her position is hopeless; that he/she is powerless over the situation. In certain situations the assurance of guilt might act to prevent an innocent suspect from providing police with an alibi for the crime or some other reasonable explanation for being implicated in the offense. Therefore, the risk is great that an innocent suspect will be charged.

The second difficulty connected to beginning a conversation with an accusation of guilt is that the book does not discuss anything to do with a proper context for the statement.

Interrogator: Since I already know that you're guilty, don't bother wasting my time by denying your guilt.
Suspect: How do you know I'm guilty?

Based on the teachings of Inbau and Reid, at that point in the conversation the interrogation will turn speechless, as the book simply does not deal with the interconnectedness between criminal investigation and custodial interrogation.

In order for police interrogation to be effective in terms of learning the truth, the interrogator must first have an excellent understanding of the case facts. Secondly, he must fully understand exactly how the suspect became linked to the crime. If both of those tasks have been done well, the interrogator should then be able to successfully explain the precise ways in which the facts of the case have led the police to the suspect. It then becomes incumbent upon the subject to offer his/her response as to an explanation to why things are actually not as they appear. All of this is based on logic and reason, so that when approached in this manner, there are only two probable outcomes: The suspect will be reasonably linked to the crime and is probably likely to confess; or the suspect will successfully convince the interrogator of the logic that he/she must be innocent.

The polygraph-interrogation link is based on the notion that guilty suspects become unnerved when in the company of the police, and therefore give away their guilt based on involuntary physical responses. This argument may stand the test as it applies to middle-class property crimes offenders, who have an active conscience and fear the law.

However, none of this applies to lower-class violent offenders, nor does it apply to serial offenders, or any other version of psychopaths. While Inbau and Reid believe in the concept of nervous offenders, those who are familiar with violent offenders have a very different frame of reference.

Violent suspects are arrested and placed in a locked interrogation room while police investigators go about their work of completing police reports, interviewing witnesses, and preparing their case for charging. During the time that the interrogator is gone, the suspect displays his general upset over having been arrested by falling sound asleep. Killers, rapists, and other violent individuals must then be coaxed to wake up and go through the booking and interrogation process. Thus, the issue of crime as normal comes into play in that the violent offender is essentially unconcerned with the proceedings. As such that type of individual is most unlikely to fail a polygraph test.

PART III

CATEGORIES OF CRIME

VIOLENT CRIME

ARTICLE 29 — *Notes on Stranger Murders*

One study on relationships between killers and their victims indicates that only 7 percent of all murders are committed by strangers. Others state that the actual percentage is somewhat greater, perhaps as much as 14 percent. The argument here would be that the percentage of murders committed by strangers is far greater than either of these estimates.

The initial problem with such relationship-related research of homicides rests in the sketchy nature of information available to researchers. To begin with, only about one-half of all murders are solved by the police. Thus one might expect that a successful police investigation might result in uncovering the nature of the relationship between the offender and victim. However, there is no reasonable way to expect that the police might be able to establish a relationship between the participants in a murder event without properly identifying the killer. Taking this one step farther, if the police know whom they are seeking, they normally would be able to locate and arrest such a person. The fact that no arrest was made implies a lack of information about motive.

Based on the validity of the above premise, it might be safely stated that in the vast majority of unsolved murders the police actually have no notion whatever as to who committed the offense, and therefore also have no idea of whether or not the victim and offender knew one another.

The question then becomes one of what percentage of cleared-by-arrest murder cases are committed by strangers. For the purposes of this discussion, let us suppose that we split the difference between the estimates of the two researchers and say that 10 percent of the solved murders were committed by strangers. The next step would then be to create a logical means of estimating what percentage of unsolved murders are the work of strangers.

A review of the literature and practical criminal investigative experience both agree that a disproportionately large percentage of murders are the work of family members, friends, and acquaintances of victims. Real and imagined issues come into play, and enraged and often intoxicated individuals lash out against persons close to them, either emotionally or geographically. Police term many such instances as "smoking gun cases," indicating that the cases are quickly solved due to the need for only the most basic level of investigation.

The result then becomes that the majority of murders solved by the police are of this type: family, friends, or acquaintances. In each instance the police look into the victim's background, find an individual with a motive to have killed the victim, and soon after the case is closed. Based on earlier limited successes in locating suspects in that manner, when new homicides come along investigators tend to reach into the only bag of tricks they know, searching for the nearby suspect with a motive to want the victim dead. The only problem with such an investigative method is that investigators with limited experience seldom look beyond that field of potential suspects. Therefore, when the crime was committed by a stranger, only one of two possible bad outcomes become possible: either the crime stands unsolved, or worse yet, the police wrongly charge an individual connected to the victim who had nothing to do with the crime.

The annals of homicide investigation are overloaded with examples of where inexperienced or poorly trained investigators wrongly charged or suspected parents of having killed their own children, or otherwise condemned suspects convenient to the case. In a later portion of this section on violent crimes, a variety of violent behaviors will be discussed, many of which should act as indicators to the police that they are likely seeking a serial killer. But for now it is sufficient to state that where overkill is present—more than one cause of death or mutilation wounds—chances are excellent that the crime was the work of a serial offender. Similarly, another trademark of the serial offender is that the actual motive for the offense is apparently known only to the killer. Lastly, when the nature of the crime indicates that the offender took a long time in carrying out the act, it is almost certainly the work of a serial killer. In such instances the joy of committing the crime far outweighs the killer's need to get away from the crime scene as quickly as possible, so as not to get caught.

Based on all of the above data, it seems quite likely that an extremely large percentage of all unsolved murders may be the work of strangers, and much of the time, strangers who are serial offenders.

ARTICLE 30 — Seeking Motives in Murder Cases

In most homicides the killer's motive becomes obvious either at the time of the crime or after the police investigation is well underway. Many times investigators feel that the most difficult part of their work is over once they have clearly established the motive for the crime. Motives may range from robbery to sexual attack to a wide variety of conflict-based issues. Obviously, at the point where police investigators have arrived at a motive for a conflict-related offense, they are equally certain that the individual with the known motive is therefore responsible for the killing. However, the reality of the issue is that because someone is extremely unhappy with an individual who later is murdered, that does not necessarily make him/her the killer.

Case Study

A successful attorney told his wife of ten years that he wanted a divorce and moved out of the family home. Soon after, the attorney was enjoying dinner at an expensive restaurant in the company of a young woman when the estranged wife approached the table and threw a plate of food in his face. She then screamed that the husband was as good as dead and she stormed out of the restaurant.

A week later the attorney was found shotgunned to death in the back seat of his own car a block away from the apartment he was renting. The wounds were to the right side of the victim's face and head. There were shotgun pellets lodged in the driver's side door. The victim's wallet was in his pants' pocket and contained $15.

The suburban police in the town where the victim was found quickly learned that the dead man had cocaine in his bloodstream. They also were informed about his estranged wife's threat made in the restaurant. She was picked up for questioning, but quickly invoked her Miranda rights and called an attorney to join her at the police station. Counsel told her to say nothing and informed the police that they needed to either charge his client or release her from custody. Authorities had no choice but to turn her loose.

From that point on police spent all of their time fitting the wife for the murder. When they learned that she had been at a cocktail party with fifty people at the time of the crime, the police simply assumed that the wife had solicited the crime to be done. In fact, they never really thought it likely that the wife had actually wielded the shotgun herself.

Weeks turned into months as the police studied their suspect's finances in search of a payment to a hired killer. They also spent long hours searching for a lover in her life who might have killed the victim on her behalf. Nothing came together which might have indicated the wife's responsibility for the crime.

Two years later the victim's siblings retained a cold case investigator to search for evidence. The new investigator quickly learned from the family that the victim had used street drugs for many years, but they had no specific information as to who he bought from or whether or not he had using friends.

The investigator went through the victim's caseload and found that he had represented only one drug dealer in the year previous to his death. The state had dropped the charges against the dealer after the victim had won a motion to suppress the police seizure of drugs from him.

The investigator met with the dealer who was difficult for the investigator to figure out. On one hand the dealer may have told the truth when he said that he had never been involved in crimes of violence, and he would not have hurt his own attorney. However, it was also noted that the dealer did seem unusually nervous at the time of their conversation. At the conclusion of their meeting, the cold case investigator got into his car and drove off leaving the dealer standing on the sidewalk.

However, others working for the investigator picked up on the dealer's trail as he moved toward his car. He drove directly to an inner-city street corner ten minutes away from where the victim's body had been found. The dealer rushed up to a large, muscular guy wearing a bandana on his head. The two moved quickly to a pearl white truck. The big guy got behind the wheel and they drove off to a bar where they took a table in the far corner away from the bar. Their discussion indicated that the two were related and that the muscular fellow had forced the dealer to set up the attorney to be robbed. All of this was overheard by those working for the cold case investigator.

Soon after, the cold case team had identified the fellow from his vehicle registration as being a recently discharged ex-convict and the half brother of the drug dealer. Numerous street informants were contacted which resulted in the following evidence coming to the surface.

The dealer had regularly supplied his attorney with user amounts of cocaine at discounted prices. He then told the victim that he had a source who would sell a pound at below wholesale price, coaxing him to the inner city. The victim was then directed into an alley at which time the half brother appeared with the shotgun and fired twice through the open passenger side window. He took the victim's money except for a few small bills, tossed him in the rear seat of his own car, and followed the dealer who led him back to the area of the victim's home. They took the victim there to divert police from the actual crime scene.

————————————

This case is an excellent example of a situation where the police were handed a murder suspect with an obviously strong motive for committing the crime. However, after hundreds of hours of investigation, they failed to locate evidence capable of linking their suspect to the crime. Many times when an investigation becomes stuck, it is simply because the initial police theory was incorrect. Hence the investigative axiom, "When stuck, start over."

Misunderstood Motives and Failed Outcomes

There is a general tendency for investigators to assume that when someone is murdered in the workplace that the offense is necessarily connected to his/her job. Police should be aware that when workplace murders are not quickly solved, the reason may be that they have miscalculated the actual motive for the crime. The following case illustrates how making an assumption as to motive can be the key determining factor in whether or not a crime is solved.

Case Study

A young woman employed as a manager of a national fast food chain was shot and killed behind a counter in the early morning hours. Case facts are as follows from a co-worker who survived the crime.

1) The victim and her employee stayed several hours past the usual closing time to prepare for a company inspection the next day.

2) As the pair was leaving the restaurant, they were approached by two men, one tall, the other short. The smaller of the two pointed a handgun stating, "You know what I want."

3) The victim then reopened the restaurant and everyone went inside.

4) The young male worker was placed inside the men's washroom and ordered to stay there.

5) Moments later the worker heard a gunshot, a scream, and what sounded like the victim falling to the floor.

6) Soon after, police responded to a burglar alarm, finding the victim dead and the helper still in the washroom.

Police learned that the money in the safe was not accessible to the killers as it was set on a time lock. A small amount of cash was still in the cash register. Police assumed that the motive had been robbery and styled their investigation based on that theory.

The following are observations of the restaurant's physical composition:

1) The building is situated across the width of the property with the customer parking lot in the front.

2) There is a clear view of the restaurant from the parking lot of an office building located directly across the road.

3) When one looks inside the restaurant windows facing the parking lot, the only view is of the dining area. Neither the

counter nor the kitchen area can be seen through the windows.

4) The kitchen is to the rear of the counter area and cannot be seen from the street.

5) The men's washroom is directly to the right of the entrance to the restaurant. Its door is kept locked.

6) Entrance to the counter and kitchen area is through a door with a keypad situated between the washroom and kitchen.

7) The only view from the outside of the building of the restaurant is from a window on the far side of the complex. Beyond that window is a ramp onto a highway.

The Usual and the Unusual

One of the first considerations surrounding any crime is whether the act took place in a routine manner, meaning whether all aspects of the offense might have been expected. For example, in this case the gunmen surfaced at a time hours later than the victim and surviving employee would normally have gone home.

This condition therefore raises the question as to whether the gunmen waited for the workers to complete their tasks or simply happened along at the time they were leaving the restaurant. If the gunmen did wait long after the employees should have gone home, just where did they wait? Two men standing in front of a closed business in the middle of the night certainly might cause police interest as would sitting in an auto in an otherwise empty parking lot. They might have also parked across the road in the office building's parking lot, which was somewhat more concealed from the road than was the restaurant.

However, there is one major problem with this consideration. Whether on foot or in an auto, the gunmen were inviting being stopped and questioned by police; and had that occurred, the gunman's weapon would have been discovered. In that instance it makes sense that the killers arrived only shortly before they expected the victim to be leaving the restaurant.

If the gunmen did not wait for the workers to leave the restaurant, then they just happened along at the time the employees were heading home and decided to confront them. The relative probability of that having taken place must be measured by certain observations; namely, that if the workers were cleaning in either the counter or kitchen areas, they could not have been seen either from the road or the parking lot as that view only allows a look at the dining room. The gunmen would have had to have occasion to look into the side window alongside the highway ramp to see the workers in the kitchen area.

Based on the above facts it seems most reasonable that the gunmen were waiting for the employees to leave the restaurant. The question then becomes one of motive. Police investigators remain of the opinion that the crime was an armed robbery attempt gone wrong. Speculation logically continues with the question of what was usual and what was not usual at the time of the murder.

On any other night the manager would have likely been leaving her job at least two hours earlier than she did on the night of her death. By applying the concept that it is probable that the gunmen did wait for them to leave work, a great question surfaces.

In what way did the late hour make the proposed armed robbery more desirable than to have committed the crime the night before or the night after?

As it happened, the strength of the robbery plan was flawed by the safe being time locked and therefore unavailable. The money drop would have taken place hours earlier before the cleaning project began if the victim followed routine policy. The question then becomes one of whether we should simply take the position that the gunmen were unaware that the funds in the safe would not be available or perhaps that the crime was totally spontaneous in nature and without any premeditation whatsoever.

Under what circumstances, then, might a situation evolve by which the shooter having killed the victim is understandable? Whether the gunmen waited for the workers to leave the restaurant or just happened upon them, they decided on forcing them back inside. Once inside, they placed the worker in the men's washroom, then walked the manager around the other side and behind the counter. Soon after, she explained that she had no access to the safe. The gunmen either became angry or perhaps panicked and shot and killed the young woman.

Though it might have happened in that manner, there are known aspects of the case which seemingly act against that theory. To begin with, murder is a big step in the sense that it greatly increases police attention above that routinely given to a simple armed robbery offense. Of far greater importance is the issue of whether it is reasonable that the killers would have at once had a reason great enough to kill the manager and at the same time decided not to also kill the employee whom they had placed in the washroom before the shooting.

While it is often risky business attempting to think along with killers, it is possible to make note of the fact that to kill one and not the other in this case is most inconsistent in nature. Whether driven by either anger or panic, it is not reasonable that the dynamics which led to the shooting was not sustained long enough to also take the life of a prospective courtroom witness. Human emotions strong enough to cause what was done to the young woman seldom instantly evaporate into thin air.

Making Determinations as to Motive

In order to believe that the victim was killed in a robbery attempt one must also

218

believe that the gunmen did embark upon that project despite the following facts:

1) There was no money to be had.
2) The restaurant workers were present when they should have been long gone.
3) They killed the victim needlessly in that they allowed a witness to the crime to live.

Facts Weighing Against a Robbery

If the crime was premeditated, it is then reasonable to assume that the gunmen knew that a clean-up project was underway which would result in the workers leaving the restaurant far later than usual. However, anyone who might have had access to that information also should have known that the safe would be time-set. Once again the issue of consistency comes into play. Just as criminal behavior would generally dictate that neither or both of the victims be killed, it is also reasonable to accept the proposition that the gunmen would have known either or both facts of the case—that the workers would be there late and that the safe was locked, or neither of them.

Within this context it will be assumed that the surviving witness is being truthful as to events. Analysis of his account of facts does nothing whatever to support the robbery theory. He first states that the small light-skinned man produced a handgun and stated, "You know what I want." Police took that statement to mean that they wanted money, however that was never said.

Is it not possible that the gunman's statement meant something entirely different to the murder victim? Certainly the gunman's words were not clearly indicative of robbery as a motive.

The worker also stated that he was placed in a washroom before his manager was shot and killed. Once again accepting that as true, at least for now, what advantage might the gunmen have enjoyed by separating the pair prior to committing an armed robbery? One thing is certain—there is very little of a secretive nature attached to the statement, "Give me your money." There is no apparent reason to deliver such a message privately. By contrast, if the gunmen had some other reason for approaching the young woman at gunpoint, they might have had the best of all reasons to wish to speak to her privately.

The most important question to be asked of the surviving worker is whether it seemed to him that the gunmen and victim seemed to have known one another. If they did know each other, then it is certain that she did know what it was that they actually wanted.

Another Theory

In a previous case study it was stated that killers moved their victim from the actual crime scene to another location in order to divert attention, which might have led to them being considered as suspects. In this case, it would have been ideal for the killer or killers to carry out the crime—or have the victim killed in her workplace, thus creating a smokescreen as to the actual motive for the crime.

A cold case investigator considered other motives for the crime and learned that the victim's husband profited handsomely from her death as the result of a corporate life insurance policy. Within a matter of days of the victim's death, the husband was involved with another woman and had purchased an expensive auto.

However, by far the most alarming fact connected to the husband was that the victim's mother died in the bathtub while getting ready to attend her child's funeral. The husband told police that his mother-in-law obviously died of a heart attack suffered due to the loss of her daughter. This account was accepted in that no investigation into the possibility that she died as a result of foul play took place.

Individuals related to the two dead women stated that it had been common knowledge that the husband had been seeing other women for the term of his marriage to the victim. Thus, a simple theory is constructed which might say that the mother confronted her son-in-law accusing him of having had the victim killed for both monetary and sexual reasons. He then did away with the danger of the mother-in-law taking her theory to the police by drowning her in the bathtub.

Whether or not this theory is accurate or not is subjective in nature. However, what is clear is that if the initial victim had been gunned down, either inside her home or near there, the husband would have been treated as a potential suspect. Then after the second death, the victim's mother in the bathtub, he would have advanced to the status of a suspect worth targeting for two separate but related murders.

ARTICLE 31 — *Understanding Violent Behavior*

The success of any given homicide investigation often depends on the investigator's ability to interpret the killer's message. Messages vary according to motive, and it is by understanding what the killer sets out to accomplish that crimes are solved. Killers who have stalked their victims prior to the murder tend to be very consistent in their behaviors. Scorned lovers act out violence in specific ways as well.

Since most individuals are killed by someone they knew, a majority of murders are solved by conducting a thorough background investigation into the victim's past, which often results in police investigators identifying a suspect with a motive. Once the motive has been established, it is often a simple matter to develop condemning evidence against the suspect.

It is far easier to solve homicides when the victim and suspect had a pre-existing relationship, if for no other reason than the limited number of potential suspects to be sifted through. By contrast, in homicides committed by strangers, the number of potential suspects is infinite. It is, therefore, easy to understand that homicide cases with such motives as robbery, sexual attack, or twisted drives known only to the killer, are far more difficult to solve than others.

What is important to understand is that few homicide offenses with differing motives tend to contain common features. For example, stalker murders tend to be extremely overt in nature in that they are typically carried out on the public way in front of countless witnesses. Standing in direct contrast are mutilation murders, where the killer often lingers about at the crime scene while slowly inflicting wounds to an already diseased victim. Both the stalker and mutilator are extreme examples of offenders driven by rage, yet they tend to act in quite opposite manners. One crime is public in nature, the other is most private. Yet, both offenses do have one common trait; neither killer seems driven by a need to escape apprehension. The stalker commits his crime in the most public manner possible, and the mutilator shows little, if any, interest in making good his getaway from the crime scene.

Violent Pasts

Regardless of the nature of the particular crime, investigators should routinely search for violent pasts among potential suspects. Virtually all killers have come to the attention of criminal justice and social justice authorities for prior violent acts. This statement is true of both juvenile and adult offenders. Violent behavior is usually a progressive condition, whereby individuals begin acting out their anger and rage in their pre-teen years. Family members, school authorities, and the police usually learn of such violent behaviors in that sequence.

Case Study

The facts of a case follow:

1) The victim was seen shopping in a super-market nearby her apartment shortly before her death.

2) An off-duty police officer saw her car being driven after she left the supermarket.

3) Several hours later, her body was found in a schoolyard. She had been raped and executed.

4) The next morning, her car was found once again parked in the supermarket lot.

5) A box-cutter—as used by supermarket employees—was found inside the car.

6) Investigators therefore considered the possibility that she had been killed by an employee of the supermarket.

There were 186 employees to be considered and interviewed. Upon conclusion of that task, the investigators treated six employees as suspects. Each consented to giving blood samples for DNA comparison, and each was thusly eliminated as the killer.

Though it is not specifically known what background information the investigating police sought of the supermarket employees, it might be rightfully assumed that they did check each potential suspect for a background of violent behavior. When an individual suspect is known to have committed acts of violence in the past, they should be considered a prime suspect until such time that the subsequent investigation clears them of the crime. Similarly, the lack of a violent past should serve as a strong indication that a given suspect is probably innocent in the pending case.

Case Study

A drive-by shooting occurred on a busy public street. The apparent target, a noted street gang member, was gunned down as were two small children playing on their bikes. Witnesses described the car as being a metallic purple Olds with neon lights all around the lower portion of the car. However, witnesses were able to provide little in the way of a description of the occupants of the car.

Police investigators did a fine job of locating an auto which fit the highly distinctive description. After conducting a short stakeout, the police were able to apprehend a young Hispanic man as he entered the purple Olds. He was arrested and taken to investigative headquarters for questioning.

The suspect stated that he knew nothing about the crime, nor had he allowed anyone else to drive his car. The police investigators responded by loudly threatening the suspect with the death penalty. That statement served to bring an end to the police questioning.

A second team of investigators was brought into the case. They soon learned that the suspect:

1) Had never been arrested for a violent act;

2) Was clearly not a member of any known street gang; and

3) Was apparently a responsible husband and father and had the same job for five years.

The new investigators made mention that the suspect's lack of a violent history—along with a lack of street gang affiliation—should be considered a huge "red flag," that he was a most unlikely prospect to be linked to a triple-murder. The initial investigators remained steadfastly convinced of his guilt, despite the only evidence against him being his purple car.

The second team of investigators convinced the suspect that they needed to know "his side of the story." It was soon learned that the suspect had been at work at the time of the crime; and before many more hours, the investigators had determined that a co-worker had lifted the car keys from the suspect's work locker, then made a duplicate set, which he passed along to his brother, an infamous street gang member. On the night of the crime, the car was taken from the employee parking lot, used in the shooting, and then returned to its original parking place. To the same extent that a violent background may act to link a guilty suspect to a crime, the lack of a violent past acts to raise serious doubt about the probability of an individual's guilt in a violent crime.

Simply put, individuals do not awake one day as teens or young adults and decide to embark upon a crime of violence for the first time. Similarly, violent behavior is enough an integral part of one's personality that it is highly improbable that such prior acts might have gone unnoticed by the authorities.

Stalking Murders

The legal terminology of stalking varies somewhat between the states; however, the following may serve to describe the act. Stalking occurs when a victim is threatened with at least one of the following:
1) Physical harm;
2) Sexual harm;
3) Physical confinement.

The threats may be either verbalized or implied. The elements of the crime are then completed when the suspect follows or watches the victim on at least two subsequent occasions.

When stalking behavior leads to murder, certain of the following characteristics of the crime may be expected to be present.
1) The crime occurs extremely quickly, usually without prior conversation on the part of the suspect.
2) The offense may occur on the public way, or often at the victim's workplace.
3) There is seldom, if ever, a sexual component to the crime.
4) A firearm is almost always the weapon used.
5) The suspect seldom formulates a plan of action to escape arrest.

Taken together, these features make it clear as to why most murders committed by stalkers are quickly solved. The usual history of a stalking incident includes prior arrests—often first for making threats—and later, for specific stalking charges. Cases dealing with such features are also often accompanied by courts issuing either a restraining order, or an order of protection, both of which are means of legally keeping the suspect geographically away from the victim. When such court orders are established, the police are notified, and therefore, authorities usually become quite familiar with the nature of the case long before the murder occurs.

In many instances, the police are able to arrest the stalking killer at or nearby the crime scene as little effort is usually made by the suspect to get away from authorities. However, when the suspect is able to make good his getaway, the police are usually able to piece together witness accounts of the crime, along with their own prior knowledge of the stalker, so that both the motive and the identity of the killer are almost immediately established. Therefore, such crimes are normally solved within a short time period, especially in comparison to other types of murders.

General Motive Crimes

Many murders are conflict-based, but lack the intense passion and rage of certain other categories of murder. Reasons for the crime may range from a neighbor parking an eyesore vehicle alongside the killer's flower garden, to a merchant raising the price of chocolate milk, or an argument over what to prepare for dinner. Most such murders are spontaneous in nature and are often a by-product of intoxication on the part of the suspect, the victim, or both.

Such crimes might occur either in a public setting, or in the privacy of a residence, and usually occur as an immediate response to the conflict. A single weapon is typically used, and the killer is usually preoccupied with hurrying from the crime scene in order to avoid detection.

Such killers generally do have violent pasts; however, the prior acts of violence tend to have also been spontaneous outbreaks—often driven by alcohol or drugs—more than other types of violent attacks such as armed robberies or sex offenses.

Incidents of domestic abuse tend to be repetitive in nature and are often fed by addiction problems. Family conflicts often continue along similar lines with the same complaints repeating themselves again and again. Each new incident adds fuel to the fire, then the addition of a state impaired by alcohol or drugs places the potential killer over the edge due to the attacker's reduced inhibitions.

This type of murder accounts for a significant percentage of all homicide incidents. They are normally easily solved as police quickly learn about the conflict which led to the crime. Such suspects also tend to readily discuss the crime with the police, so confessions are common.

Robbery-Related Murders

Within the criminal subculture, status is awarded based on the nature of the deviant acts committed by its members. Just as musical prowess and athletic achievements are sources of pride and recognition, so is the work of the criminal. The more daring the crime, the greater is one's status within the criminal community. Within this framework, the work of the armed robber is placed just below that of only the police-killer in terms of esteem and recognition from street criminals.

The term used on the street for exhibiting courage or nerve in the course of the commission of criminal acts is "heart." The individual who packs a firearm and enters the supermarket and leaves with the contents of the safe possesses great heart. The task of armed robbery requires the suspect to be willing to confront danger. Though the robber himself is armed, it is implicit in the act that the risk of the robber being shot and killed, either by a resistant victim or by responding police, is always present. Within the criminal milieu, the greater the perceived risk attached to committing the crime, the greater the status afforded to the offender.

That robbers hold high status within the criminal community is best illustrated by the fact that it is common for robbers to take snapshots of the loot successfully taken in robberies, along with the weapons and other items used in the crime, such as ski masks. The photos are then placed prominently on display as a means of memorializing the successful robbery.

Other criminals who commit less daring offenses are seen as clearly less than the equal of those with "heart." That means, among other things, that they are not allowed to congregate on the same segment of the street with home-invaders, stick-up men, and other shooters.

Wise criminals understand certain aspects of police behavior. They know, for example, that the police work far harder and longer on robberies in which a victim has been seriously injured or killed, than they do in routine offenses where only property loss has been suffered. Therefore, most armed robbers harm their victims only when they feel forced to do so, usually due to resistance on the part of the victim.

Robbery is defined as taking property from the person of another by either a threat of force, or by actual use of force. Armed robbery occurs when the suspect is armed with a dangerous weapon in the course of that crime. Home invasion is a term used to describe the armed robbery of individuals inside a dwelling. Carjacking is an act of robbery or armed robbery in which the property taken is a motor vehicle.

Robbery investigation centers on investigators getting to know a large segment of the total pool of offenders. By gathering mug shots of known offenders, it is possible for the police investigator to obtain a photo identification of the suspect, sometimes within a matter of moments after the commission of an offense. It then becomes a simple matter of locating the suspect who is then arrested and placed in a police line-up for the purpose of gaining a positive, in-person identification, which is usually adequate evidence to get the suspect charged. This investigative process is made easier by the fact that most inner-city robbers do not move about to commit their crimes. Most robberies are committed by suspects who reside in the immediate area of the offense.

However, robbery murders are often the work of a small segment of armed robbers who have a sadistic side and will injure or kill their victims upon completion of the robbery aspect of the crime, even when the victim follows the robber's directions to the letter.

A second issue that makes many investigations difficult rests in the fact that there is an entirely different set of robbery-murders in which robbery is not the primary motive for the crime, but rather it is merely an after thought to killing the victim.

Case Study

A young woman was found murdered in her motel room in Santa Fe, New Mexico. She was resting face-down on a bed with her hands bound behind her with strips of a torn pillow case. She suffered a major stab wound in the back and multiple stab wounds to the neck.   The motel room had not been ransacked, and the killer did not take the keys to her car or to the U-Haul trailer, which contained most of her belongings.   A certain amount of cash remained in her purse, and some of the jewelry was still in place. However, some cash and several pieces of jewelry were taken in the course of the crime. Thus, there was a robbery element to the crime, yet robbery clearly was not the killer's primary motive.

The ability to recognize primary motive is key toward case solution, as an investigative decision to center the investigation of the murder on known armed robbers would likely have been extremely time-consuming and would have ultimately been a fruitless endeavor.

Crimes with a Sexual Component

Sex offenders may generally be categorized according to one primary aspect of method of operation, whether they carry out their acts out of doors on the public way or in the course of illegal entries into a dwelling. Though sex offenders are compulsive criminals who tend to continually act out until caught by authorities, they nonetheless seldom stray from a single method of operation.

Case Study

In the course of investigating the murder of a young woman in her apartment, the investigator searched for other possible crimes that might have been committed by her killer. It was learned that over Memorial Day weekend in 1978, another young woman named Rita was killed in a train station slightly more than a mile south of where the victim was later killed inside her apartment. Rita's attacker had apparently confronted her with a knife and forced her to disrobe from the waist down; however, before the actual sex attack could occur, he was interrupted by the arrival of another passenger to the train station. The attacker mortally wounded the intruder, then chased and stabbed Rita to death.

The killer was never caught, however that is not to say that police lacked clues and leads to follow. The day after the murder, a suspect who closely resembled the killer hopped a fence into a yard and raped a woman as she sunbathed. Over the succeeding years, more than thirty other women were sexually attacked by a suspect who was described as clean-cut in appearance, and who engaged his victims in intelligent, refined conversation.

What are most significant are issues of method of operation. The offenses all took place out of doors during warm-weather months between May and October. The six-year-long pattern of crimes culminated in August, 1984, with the rape-murder of Kathleen, who was killed as she went jogging only blocks away from her home. Witnesses told police that as she moved toward an alley where the crime took place, the clean-cut suspect dressed in jogging gear began trailing her on foot. Ten minutes later, they heard screams coming from the alley, and the victim's body was found.

Investigators assigned to Kathleen's case readily admitted to the press that the description of the killer was "practically identical to that of a rapist who had struck four times in the late-summer of 1982 in precisely the same area where the jogger was killed. What they did not say, however, was that the description of the suspect was also identical to that of a multiple sex offender who had been given the name of "jogger rapist" after having committed a dozen offenses during the late-summer of 1978.

Case Analysis

As discussed elsewhere, it is quite possible that the same individual killed both Rita and Kathleen. Their having been killed in the course of an intended sexual attack would be in keeping with the suspect's general method of operation. In the first incident, it is clear that the intended sexual attack of Rita was not consummated only because of the suspect being interrupted by the arrival of the second victim. Hypothetically, the same suspect might have committed scores of sexual offenses as suggested, and none of those would have led to the murder of the victim, providing that the suspect kills only when he meets resistance. This possible theory is imperfect to the extent that the actual dynamics of the interaction between the suspect and Kathleen in the alley where she was attacked is not known.

In the event that she complied with the knife-wielding suspect's orders and was killed anyway, then the probability is that her killer was not the serial rapist who allowed his many rape victims to live. However, she failed to follow directions, or physically resisted, then the theory that one individual killed both young women remains sound. Similarly, a variation of the same concept might have been that a third person might have come along, as in Rita's case, and in some way interrupted the crime.

The concept of suspects attacking their victims is well-founded within the study of robbery offenders. A small percentage will not harm their victims even if they were to meet great resistance. Those offenders are simply not well-suited for the task of armed robbery and would themselves flee before they might turn a weapon on their victim. The largest groups of robbers wish for their criminal work to go smoothly and, therefore, do not wish to injure their victims, for they know that the police investigate such crimes with far greater intensity than more routine robberies where nobody has been injured. This category of robber will bring physical harm to their victim only when they meet resistance. This typology of robbers is completed by the sadist who first warns his victim against resistance, gains the victim's compliance, and then injures or kills them anyway.

There are the same types among sex offenders as well. The same offender might have killed both women because of having been met with some form of resistance, but also might have carried out the countless other sexual attacks in between in which none of those victims were either injured or killed. Within the eyes of the suspect, there was no reason to use his knife on victims who did just as they were told. There exists, however, another type of sex offender who accounts for a large percentage of serial killers. Their description follows shortly.

This theory dealing with a serial rapist and killer gains support from both the common physical description of the suspect, along with a common method of operation in that all of the crimes took place out of doors and during warm-weather months. Unfortunately, the validity of the theory remains largely a matter of speculation in that no cold case investigation has taken place, which might either prove the theory to be unsound or lead to the identification of the suspect.

Summary of Killer Categories

In general terms, about one-half of all the homicides are cleared by arrest each year in the United States. While it is impossible to determine just what percentage of murders from each of the categories discussed are actually solved, it is safe to state that more than one-half of the categories of killers discussed above are solved.

The simple fact that most homicide victims are killed by someone they knew makes those cases easier to solve than others. Robbery-murders are often solved by virtue of the fact that such killers often openly brag about their work, which results in an informant sharing that information with the police. Stalkers are nearly always caught in that their past threats toward their victim stands as loud evidence of motive once the stalking turns to murder. Sex offenders who killed due to their victim's resistance, or some other complicating factor are usually also caught simply because sex offenders comprise such a small pool of criminal suspects. If a given community might have five active rapists working in the area, there are probably fifty or more robbers. It is therefore by sifting through a very limited number of potential suspect that rape-murder of this type is solved.

These are the "easy" murders to solve. Since most homicide investigations identify one of the above categories of suspects as the wanted individual, it is logical that most police investigators focus on such types to solve whatever homicide they are investigating. However, a significantly large percentage of the homicides that are never solved do not fit into any of the above categories, and that may be the very reason that they are not solved.

Murders without Obvious Motive

Most killers know their victims. Most killers hurry through the commission of the crime in order to place distance between themselves and their crime. And, in many murders, the killer speaks of his motive through significant facts surrounding both the crime scene and the manner in which the crime was accomplished.

However, a very large percentage of homicides which come to the attention of cold case investigators are appreciably different than crimes previously discussed. They are unlike other offenses in at least some of the following ways:

1) Wounds to the victim often imply that the killer was not in any hurry to flee the crime scene.
2) More than one cause of death is often employed.
3) Though there is often a sexual aspect of the crime, many times there are no signs of a struggle, and only semen within the victim suggests a rape has occurred.
4) The crime scene is often tidy, as if the victim had been entertaining a friend.
5) Certain property may be taken, yet other valuables are often left behind.
6) There is often no damage to entrances to the crime scene, an indication that the victim allowed the killer inside.
7) The killer often tells the victim that if he/she complies with instructions, he/she will save his/her life.

8) The killer then betrays the victim by killing him/her, despite a lack of resistance.

In many such cases, certain of these features will be present. Many times there will also be other unusual aspects of the crime which escape the above list. However, when some combination of the above qualities is present in a homicide, it is safe to take the position that the actual motive for the offense is simply the job the killer derives from committing the act itself.

Four primary cases are treated in this book. They are remarkable for the number of apparent similarities as to the behaviors of their respective killers.

In the first case the victim was killed in her studio apartment. She had been beaten about the head, with at least one blunt instrument, strangled, and had over forty other superficial wounds to her torso, including a bite mark to the left shoulder and two strangely configured puncture wounds to the back. She had semen in her vaginal track, but no other signs of sexual attack.

A Bible student contacted the police to tell them about his having had a dream about a similar attack at the same time that his neighbor was being killed two doors away. He was charged with the rape and murder, convicted of the murder, and sentenced to forty years in prison. Ten years later, the state dropped all charges against him on the eve of a re-trial ordered by an appeals court.

The nature and extent of multiple wounds strongly indicates that the victim was killed by the type of suspect who commits many murders that come to the attention of cold case investigators—the killer with a motive known only to himself.

The second victim was raped and murdered inside a motel room in Santa Fe, New Mexico, in 1983. She had been strangled, stabbed in the back through her sweater, and stabbed multiple times in the neck. At the time the body was discovered, she was dressed except for her bra, and her hands were bound behind her back, and remarkably, she, too, had a bite mark in precisely the same location as the one inflicted on the first victim.

For more than a decade, the family was told by the police that there simply were no leads, which led to a cold case investigation in 1995. It was quickly learned that there were actually multiple suspects, none of which had ever been properly eliminated by the police.

The third victim was a young accountant for the CIA in Washington, D.C. Her naked body was found alongside her neatly folded clothes in a schoolyard in the early morning hours in May, 1988. She had been raped and executed, shot point-blank in the face with a handgun.

This case was featured on the television production, *Unsolved Mysteries*. Though their treatment of the case depicted a handsome stranger the victim had apparently just met in a supermarket as the killer, the baffled police investigators stated that they remained convinced that the victim had been killed by a jilted lover from the victim's home state of Oklahoma.

In both the first and second cases, the police focused their attention on "convenient" suspects who failed to meet the profiles of individuals who go about killing in the manner of those crimes. The Bible student was wrongly charged in the first case, despite the fact that he had absolutely no known history as a violent offender. His having contacted the police about his alleged dream simply made him an easy suspect. In the supermarket case, the police had clearly misinterpreted case facts, failed to follow logical leads, and therefore, conveniently claimed that the crime had been committed by someone located two thousand miles away, where the police could not be expected to know about them.

The killers in all three cases seemingly sought out their respective victims for the deliberate purpose of murder and rape. All three killers took great risks in the commission of their crimes: In two cases they took an exhaustive amount of time engaged in "overkill" behaviors when most other suspects would have been preoccupied with getting away from the crime scene. In the supermarket (third) case, the killer risked discovery by having first been seen with the victim inside the supermarket, then by forcing her into her own car at gunpoint, and driving her toward her eventual death. Her killer was observed by an off-duty police officer between the supermarket and the crime scene, yet he chose a tactic designed to outsmart the officer, rather than to relinquish custody of his victim and flee, as most suspects would do.

A prime example of the need for a serial killer to become adaptive to his compulsions to kill is prominent in the behavior of the killer seven months after the victim's death.

Just as the third victim's killer spotted her in her red shoes, then was driven to attack and kill her, he later was drawn to his next victim for the same reason. So great was his compulsive rage to take her life that he undertook the major complication that she was with her boyfriend at the time.

Undeterred, he kidnapped the couple at gunpoint and forced them to drive to an isolated area where he executed the boyfriend with a single shot to the back of the head. As the female attempted fleeing on foot, she too was shot in the head before being sexually attacked.

Remarkably, the police ignored that both women wore red shoes and that both had their clothes neatly stacked alongside their bodies. They took the position that the crimes were unrelated primarily because this victim had been with her boyfriend when killed. Unfortunately, what was lost on the police was the adaptive nature of serial killers to modify their preferred method of operation in order to carry out their "need" to kill.

It should be understood that killers of this ilk commit their crimes simply for the job of the act. Once this basic fact is understood, it is also possible to accept that the time-consuming aspects of their crime do not concern this type of killer as they would others. For them, the risk of being caught simply enhances their pleasure based on their ability to avoid investigative scrutiny. Mutilation and other overkill aspects of such crimes are the basis for this killer's need to act out in the first place. To inflict any less wounds would leave them short of the satisfaction commission of the act provides them. Similarly, the more time taken in the course of the crime, the greater their satisfaction at having outsmarted the police.

Such killers respond to twisted quirks which act to "trigger" their behaviors. To the extent that they are triggered to act, it is a safe assumption that this is not something that is likely to occur only once. If the long, black curly hair of a victim caused her killer to experience an inner rage and respond by committing the crime as a result, there are clearly going to be other women—and similar conditions—where the same suspect will respond in the same manner to such stimuli and, therefore, act out in the same manner with a different victim. Make no mistake about it, to the extent that this category of killer is impulsively "triggered" to act, the behavior will be repeated in similar fashion until caught.

The Search

While there is certain to be a common thread between one crime and the next, the impulsive killer's method of operation may be less constant than among other criminal offenses. For example, if an armed robber has had success in robbing taxi drivers while posing as a passenger leaving a train station, he may use that tact time after time. The robber is able to make a logical decision to commit another robbery which results in his gathering his weapon and setting out for the place in which he has decided to identify a potential victim, and then carry out the crime in keeping with his chosen method of operation. This offender has the luxury of such extensive planning.

The impulsive killer's plight is totally different. For example, in the third case, it seems apparent that her killer saw the victim as she walked from the parking lot and into the supermarket. The killer's particular "trigger" seems to have been the red shoes the victim wore. Her shoes, perhaps along with the victim's general appearance, thus compelled the killer to act. He then entered the supermarket with a clear-cut plan in mind to rape the victim in the course of taking her life. Since the killer was emotionally lured to his intended victim, he did not have the luxury of the more logically inclined criminal who is able to map out a specific course of action in advance of the crime. This category of offender is forced to improvise as he moves toward the culmination of his criminal act. It is for this reason that essentially similar crimes committed by a single offender may seem on the surface to be different as the result of differing methods of operation.

When the impulsive killer acts, it should therefore be an investigative expectation that each possible serial offense will have differing aspects to them due to the spontaneous nature of having responded to something the killer saw in a potential victim.

Searching for Triggers

It is an investigative error to assume that the victims of impulsive killers are likely to all be of the same race or the same physical size or of the same age group. The psychological quirks which may activate the killer might be something as deeply hidden as the fragrance of a perfume once worn by an abusive individual, or a facial expression of someone who may, or may not, actually resemble an individual in the killer's past.

It is a common investigative error to dismiss the possibility that one suspect may have committed multiple offenses. In the third case, the police remained convinced that she was killed by a former lover, despite the fact that another young woman was killed in a similar way a short distance away seven months later. Investigators decided that two major differences between the respective cases were sufficient to assume against the presence of a common killer. The third victim was African-American, while the fourth victim was white. The fourth victim was killed along with her boyfriend, while the third victim had been alone.

However, what was constant in both cases was that both of the female victims wore red shoes, and the clothing of both females was nearly folded alongside the place where they were raped and met their death. It was not until nearly a decade later that DNA conclusively proved that the same suspect had raped—and therefore killed—both women.

Crime Location

One usual characteristic of a method of operation is the location where the crime takes place. As stated earlier, rapists usually either work indoors or outdoors. Some suspects grab their victims as they walk past the mouth of the alleys or as they enter or exit their autos in or near garages. Others lurk in the vestibules of apartment buildings in wait of potential victims to open a door toward their apartment.

A different manner of sex offender attacks after having entered a victim's home, either by means of burglary or home invasion. Police investigators have learned that very few sex offenders—who allow their victims to live after the attack—change methods of operation by committing the crimes both indoors and outdoors. They are like armed robbers in that they have the luxury of planning their crimes in such a way that they can be certain of just what the crime scene will be like.

The impulsive killer makes no such plans, any more than he can effectively predict just when he will be triggered toward committing another crime. It is, therefore, quite possible that one such offense might occur outside in a park, the next inside where he might have followed his victim, to be stalked by yet another attack inside an abandoned auto. The impulsive killer improvises toward the successful commission of his crime. This is therefore yet one more example of the ways in which a simple study of method of operation may totally obscure the fact that various seemingly dissimilar crimes are actually the work of a single serial killer.

Investigative Guidelines

When an overkill murder, especially one with a sexual component, is discovered, the probability is great that the suspect has killed others in the past in a way, which is at least somewhat similar. *All murders in which the suspect seems to have spent a great deal of time in the course of the act should be scrutinized.* Differences in method of operation should be disregarded, and a search should center upon seeking as little as one similarity between the various crimes.

All time-consuming homicides with a sexual overtone should be considered as the work of a serial killer.

Perhaps the single most important guideline in conducting such investigations is that any two overkill crimes committed within short proximity of one another are probably the work of a single killer. The worst thing any investigator—cold case or otherwise—can ever do is to make an arbitrary decision that the cases are unrelated without first having thoroughly investigated both crimes. The probability is overwhelmingly great that the search is actually for a serial killer.

Wounds as a Method of Operation

Despite the impulsive killer's dilemma of often having to improvise along the way as his crime is developing, there are certain killers whose crimes will bear a "trademark" in terms of the manner and nature of wounds inflicted upon the victim. Some examples are as common as strangulation by means of the victim's blouse or scarf being twisted around the neck. In other cases, the wounds may be so unusual that they set the case apart from virtually all others.

For example, the victim in the second case was stabbed multiple times in the neck. Though knife wounds to the neck are common, they are normally in the form of lacerations, thus the term "slitting one's throat." Therefore, when police gained information that another young woman in a neighboring state was also killed by stab wounds to the neck, that killer rightfully should have been considered a prime suspect in the second case.

Case Study

A young woman was found in the warm-up house of an ice-skating rink in a well-known winter resort area. She had been strangled with a long scarf she wore around her neck. Her ski pants were in place; however, her panties were found in the woman's washroom nearby. The autopsy disclosed a presence of semen within her vaginal track, but there was no other evidence supportive of rape. There were more than sixty puncture wounds to the front of her torso, and the victim's long, blonde hair was tied together in a tight knot in a haphazard manner.

Police investigators looked into the victim's past and found that she had broken up with an individual who had continued to pursue her for many months after. He had no clear-cut alibi for the time of the crime, claiming to have been home alone at the time that the victim was killed several hundred miles away. Police spent several days attempting to locate service station attendants or train personnel who might have been able to place the suspect near the crime scene; however, no such witnesses were to be found. Investigators then subjected the former boyfriend to a rigorous line of questioning, however, the suspect continued to maintain his innocence.

Months went by, during which time the police obtained the suspect's telephone records and maintained extensive surveillance of him, in hopes that he might do something to give away his guilt.

The case went unsolved for several years. The victim's family then retained a cold case investigator, who soon noted that the victim had been to a beauty salon during the last day of her life. A visit was made there at which time it was learned that the stylist who had done the victim's hair had long since moved out of state, therefore, it was not immediately possible to learn about the nature of the victim's conversation while having her hair done.

The owner of the salon, however, clearly recalled the victim having been there. The new investigator then asked whether she might recall anything unusual about the day in question. She responded that the crime took place during a stretch of time in which a "very strange homeless type" had been hanging around on the bench next to the salon. It seems that he had attempted to strike up a conversation with certain salon customers as they came and went. Salon clients were afraid of him and called the police.

What was most significant about the conversation was that the salon owner was positive that she never saw the stranger again after the murder. The investigator inquired as to whether she had shared the same information with the original investigators. She stated that she had never been interviewed until that very day.

A few pieces of information had surfaced:

1) A suspect whose behavior and demeanor were sufficient to scare women had been lurking about prior to the crime;

2) A salon might have served as a place for the killer to effectively "scout" women, and;

3) He was never again seen in the area after the murder.

The new investigator had both the best and worst of it: He had a strong lead to follow, however, he also faced the difficult task of attempting to identify and locate an unknown suspect. Clearly, someone in the area was likely to have known something about the stranger at the time of the crime. But it would be a seemingly impossible task to move about the immediate community asking questions about a nameless suspect years after the fact. Note the recurring nature of this problem.

The police were contacted. In a stroke of good luck, a female officer did recall the vagrant; however, no official report was filed which might contain the suspect's name. He was a homeless drifter with bad hygiene, and the only other thing the officer recalled about him was that he said that he was from Iowa. He was white, age about thirty at the time, and had a pockmarked face. The new investigator spent several more days in the area of the salon seeking more information about the suspect, but none was forthcoming.

Iowa police were told about the case. They had no leads as to the suspect; however, they did have information about an unsolved rape and murder in which the victim was apparently abducted from a public telephone in front of a convenient store. In that case, the victim was stabbed multiple times with an unknown type of weapon, which inflicted puncture wounds. The cold case investigator was also able to determine that the semen in the Iowa victim was of the same blood typing as in the initial case. This information would be sufficient to assume that both crimes were committed by the same suspect until actual DNA typing could be accomplished.

A search was then undertaken for the suspect in shelters and other places where the homeless congregate. At each stop along the way, the investigator asked about an individual who might have been reluctant to put down his knapsack or duffel bag. At perhaps the tenth stop, an elderly woman at a soup kitchen asked how in earth it was that he knew that about a fellow. She explained that only a few months earlier just such an individual attacked another homeless person for having picked up his travel bag. "Stuck him good with an ice pick, he did," she said.

As it turned out, the victim had refused to sign a complaint, however, the suspect's name was on file with the local police. Thus, the hunt for Julius Wilkes was on.

By then, it was early-May and warm weather landed in a college town the same day the cold case investigator arrived. He cruised in and out of paths leading to and from sorority houses before focusing on an individual who might have been Wilkes. He sat on a park bench leering at certain of the passing coeds. To be precise, the suspect leered only at the girls who were blonde. The investigator took a hundred-dollar bill and poked a hole through it with a stick, then stuck it into the law a few feet away from where the suspect sat. It only took a few seconds for the suspect to see the money and lunge toward it. At that instant, the investigator grabbed the dirty green bag from the bench. Inside it was an ice pick and a blonde wig with its long, fake hair tied into a knot, just like had been done to both victims in the course of their attacks.

When Julius saw his belongings spread out on the bench, he stood spellbound and began hyperventilating as handcuffs were placed on his wrists. Within a day or two, more "overkill" crimes were uncovered in nearby states. The suspect admitted to all of them.

The killer's "trigger" was formed by his first girlfriend who, after introducing him to lovemaking, mocked him by telling him about her many other lovers. His plan to kill her had become spoiled when she committed suicide, so Julius was forced to take up his cause on other attractive young women with long, blonde hair. His chosen method of operation was so vital to his crimes that he carried his weapon with him everywhere he went so that he might be "prepared" when just the right victim triggered him into action. Similarly, he carried the blonde wig with him, both as a constant reminder of his "cause," and also so that he might practice knotting the hair of his victims just so.

Case Study

A man was killed inside a steam room within the men's locker room of a posh health club. The victim was one of four individuals in the steam room when two others walked in. They sat alongside the victim. Seconds later, one of the new arrivals turned toward the victim and told him that he was not supposed to be shaving in the steam room. Witnesses would later state that there was then an angry reply, apparently from the victim. One of the men who had just entered the room smashed the victim's head against the tile wall, killing him instantly. The two suspects then walked from the steam room.

Witnesses stated that the room had been too steamy to see the faces of the suspects. Investigators interviewed scores of individuals seeking information about possible suspects who might have been seen dressing quickly after the crime. They also inquired about members or guests known to have bad tempers, and they inspected guest lists. They also searched for witnesses who might have seen strangers sneaking into the club. The investigators also looked into the back-grounds of club employees, seeking someone with a violent history who might have "flipped out" at the victim having been shaving in the steam room. Months later, the case remained unsolved.

The commander of the investigative unit then reassigned the case to a different team. They read the police file and immediately saw that the initial investigators had never moved beyond searching for clues centered on the health club and the killers' apparent violent reaction to the victim's practice of shaving in the steam room.

The new investigators did a thorough background check of the victim and soon learned that there were at least two parties who might have had a motive for killing him. According to the victim's mother, the widow had done very little grieving and was currently seeing a much younger fellow. The victim had also sued a former business partner only days before having been killed.

However, the notion that the victim had been killed for any reason other than the apparent conflict inside the steam room flew directly in the face of known case facts. Others inside the steam room were most certain that the altercation had seemingly been the result of a simple violation of the no shaving policy.

The new investigators began by attempting to create a theory which might account for the apparent events inside the locker room. By now, the disposable razor had been worked on at the crime laboratory.

The victim's fingerprints had survived the steam of the crime scene, and the whiskers on it were also his. An examination of the crime scene photos clearly disclosed that the victim's face was completely shaved.

The investigators then constructed the following hypothesis to account for the case facts: Two individuals had reason to kill the victim which had nothing to do with shaving, however, they wished not to be caught for the crime and therefore devised a plan which might divert police attention toward a false motive.

The killers would have been familiar with the victim's schedule at the health club. They watched the victim shave. He then did one of three things with the dirty razor; he might have tossed it into the trash container, or left it atop the sink counter after finishing his shave, or perhaps he placed it back into his gym bag which was sitting beside his locker after the crime was discovered.

In any event, the killers retrieved the razor, handling it with a tissue so as not to leave their own prints and not to destroy those of the victim. The pair then followed the victim into the steam room, and then sat beside him. One suspect made the statement cautioning against shaving in the steam room, then the other suspect responded, making an angry comment of his own. The killers then immediately smashed the victim's head against the wall before he might speak. Witnesses inside the room would have logically assumed that the reply had come from the victim and not from the suspect sitting only inches away from him. The killers then dropped the victim's razor at his feet and walked out of the steam room.

It might have happened that way and would have reasonably caused the investigators to search based on a motive that did not exist. For just as long as investigators continued to focus only on that faulty motive, the crime would remain all but impossible to solve.

The new investigators then looked carefully into the background of the victim's former business associate. There was nothing in his past to indicate a violent or otherwise criminal past. When interviewed by investigators, he stated in a matter-of-fact way that he would easily win the lawsuit which, was still pending, despite the death of the victim.

The investigators then looked into the widow as a possible suspect. They soon determined that she had been frequenting a certain bar located in a nearby hotel, and that she had struck up a friendship with a known member of organized crime. The finances of the victim and widow were researched, and it was learned that several thousands of dollars had been withdrawn by the widow a week before her husband's death.

Investigators then gathered photos of known associates of the organized crime figure the widow had been seen with at the bar. They were then placed in a photo gallery and shown to employees of the health club where the murder had occurred. Both front desk and membership employees identified two suspects as having been given a tour of the club at about the same time as the steam room murder.

The widow was then confronted with that information and quickly admitted to having put together a murder-for-hire scheme, which two members of organized crime cleverly carried out by providing police investigators with a false motive in which to become lost.

Chances of identifying the actual motive are greatly enhanced by objective, open-minded viewing of the killer's actions. Above all else, when stuck, start over.

In general terms the offense of theft places very limited requirements on its actors. Random theft offenses are based largely on opportunity and little else. An individual observes an unguarded item of some value, quickly sizes up the surroundings, then makes a decision that there is little if any chance of detection. Such acts are in no way based on seeking out valuable items to cash in on, nor does the act call for any specialized skills on the part of the offender.

One step removed from the totally opportunistic thief is the offender who actively seeks unguarded items to steal, or items that may be taken with limited effort due to their accessibility. The stealing of personal items left in unlocked vehicles is a good example of this category of theft. In such instances, the only requirement on the part of the offender is to look inside the vehicle and then run the limited risk of pulling open the unlocked door and removing the item to be taken. This offense is typically a low-risk, low-reward offense in that the task of stealing is made easy by the fact that the vehicle was left unlocked. However, items most often left inside an unlocked vehicle are of very limited value.

Theft of auto accessories, usually CD/ stereo sets, require both a greater risk on the part of the offender and also a bit of knowledge as to how to break into the vehicle and then quickly separate the items to be taken from the vehicle. Without training and experience it would be difficult to pop a stereo from the dashboard before being noticed. This offense is therefore a much higher-risk offense that the theft of personal items from vehicles, however the rewards are also far greater based on the relatively high value of the electronic equipment taken.

Theft offenders do not enjoy high status within the criminal subculture. The lack of violence involved in their criminal acts excludes them from mixing as equals with robbers, home invaders, and carjackers, all of whom typically threaten the use of violence or do exact violence in the commission of their crimes. The comparison, as seem through the eyes of the criminal subculture, is that violent acts require daring, while thefts require nothing more than sneaky behavior.

Enticement, Entrapment, and Theft Offenses

Police entrapment occurs when the police create a situation whereby an individual commits a criminal act which they would not have otherwise committed. Entrapment is therefore an affirmative defense, whereby the accused states, "Yes, I did it but only because the police entrapped me."

By comparison, enticement occurs when the police create a situation which simply allows the criminal the opportunity to do whatever it is that he/she intended to do in the first place. The distinction between enticement and entrapment may be best illustrated by this non-theft example.

Case Problem

Police combat street prostitution by placing undercover female officers in the role of prostitutes for the purpose of arresting the men who proposition them. If the officer simply stands on the street and allows passing men to offer her money for sex, this is enticement and the act is legal. However, if the undercover officer waves at men on the street or makes the first approach upon prospective customers, this is entrapment, in that the behavior of the officer might cause someone to engage in a criminal behavior that he would not have otherwise committed.

A great deal of police enticement and entrapment centers on theft enforcement. For example, police may place a seemingly drunk undercover officer in a train station late at night. If the officer pretends to be asleep and simply allows an individual to approach and remove property from his pocket, the act would be enticement and thus legal. However, if the officer once again pretended to be asleep in the train station and had a $50 bill sticking halfway out of his shirt pocket, the act would become entrapment in that the presence of the money nearly falling from the decoy's pocket would create a situation where an individual who had no inclination to steal might seize the opportunity to take the money.

Another example of enticement versus entrapment might concern theft of personal property from a vehicle. If the items designed to get the attention of a thief were simply set on the front seat of what appeared to be a secured auto, this would be police enticement in that it offered a thief the chance to steal. By contrast, if the items of value were in plain view of anyone walking by the car with its windows rolled down, the act would be considered an act of entrapment, in that all that would be required was to reach inside the open window and take the valuables.

The fact that such police decoy operations frequently take place is a strong indication of just how strong the power of suggestion is for opportunistic offenders to engage in theft.

ARTICLE 33 — *Felony Theft Offenses*

In most states, whether a theft constitutes a misdemeanor or felony offense is determined by the value of the item taken. In some jurisdictions below $350 is a misdemeanor, above that amount is a felony.

There is also another distinction regarding the level of offense in that theft from a person is always a felony. The lawmakers' thinking is that when an offender and potential victim are in close proximity to one another, the danger exists that something will go wrong in the course of the theft attempt, which might lead to a physical confrontation. When such interactions become physical, the victim's safety becomes a concern. Therefore purse-snatching, pick-pocketing, and snatch-and-grab thefts are typically felony offenses.

Purse-snatching takes on certain behaviors connected to street robberies. In both instances potential victims are scouted and approached. As opposed to the robber who uses either a weapon, force, or the threat of force, the purse-snatcher uses the element of surprise. The victim is approached from the rear, run up upon, and the victim's bag is reached for. When the offender is accomplished, the purse comes free easily and the offender simply continues his run past the victim toward safety. In this ideal situation, the victim is unharmed except for the loss of her property. Should that offender be apprehended by authorities, he will be charged with felony theft from a person.

The dangers inherent in theft from a person surfaces when something goes wrong in the course of the crime. Perhaps the victim hears the offender approaching and braces herself, causing resistance at the point of the offender's grabbing action. In other instances, women may wrap their purse strap around their arm. When that occurs, the victim is typically knocked down by the force of the grabbing action, thus what began as a theft becomes a robbery due to the force used in the act.

In pick-pocketing offenses there are far more offenders attempting to ply that craft than are actually accomplished offenders. Therefore in many such attempts the victim realizes what the offender is attempting to do, and resists accordingly. Even when the physical contact is initiated by the victim, often in an attempt to subdue the offender for the police, what began as a theft from a person turns into a robbery.

Case Study

An art thief removed a painting from a wall and removed it from its frame. He then rolled it up and began walking toward the museum exit. He was intercepted by a security officer, who attempted to detain the offender. The thief responded by grabbing a large vase on display and breaking it over the officer's head in an attempt to make good his getaway. The offender fled the museum but was quickly located and arrested by responding police.

The charges were armed robbery and aggravated battery. When an offender who has committed a theft uses force to make good his/her attempted flight to freedom, the initial offense is upgraded accordingly. If physical force is used, the enhanced offense becomes robbery. If, as in this case study, a weapon is used, the offense becomes armed robbery.

Snatch-and-grab thefts are frequently committed acts. There are two basic categories of this offense, the first being where an offender will reach into the open window of an auto stopped at a red light and grab personal belongings from the seat. Far more frequently offenders will approach potential victims wearing jewelry around their neck, and simply grab it and run off. When the snatch-and-grab theft concerns property within an auto, the offense is a misdemeanor. Grabbing jewelry from an individual's neck is theft from a person and a felony offense.

ARTICLE 34 — *Shoplifting and Addiction*

Certain major city court systems have drug courts, which attempt to place addicted offenders in treatment or 12-Step programs. Drug courts have been quite successful in that individuals who take recovery seriously tend to stay clean and therefore abandon their old criminal ways. Once drug use discontinues, usually so does the accompanying criminal behavior.

Large court systems also attempt to classify criminal offenders through other specialized courts. For example, for several decades Cook County (Illinois) had had gun court, auto theft court, and domestic relations court, as well as shoplifting court.

Criminologists have engaged in much research dealing with shoplifting (retail theft), finding that about 15 percent of all thefts are incidents of shoplifting. An equal percentage of active shoplifters are both male and female. About 41 percent are white, 29 percent are Black, and 16 percent Hispanic. Research also indicates that 8 percent of all retail customers are shoplifters. Lastly, it is estimated that only 10 percent of all shoplifters are classified as professionals.

This figure was considered and did not seem realistic in terms of other data accepted as valid regarding criminal behavior. For example, it has been accepted as common knowledge that addicted criminals typically support their drug habits either through prostitution and pandering, or by theft.

Moreover, it is commonly believed that shoplifting is perhaps the most popular form of theft to the addicted professional offender due to its reliable nature. Overall, theft is often an opportunistic offense in that an individual views an unguarded item of value and observes that conditions indicate that to steal the item would be a low-risk proposition. However, the addicted offender has an ongoing need to steal in order to get money to buy drugs. Thus he/she does not have the luxury of waiting for periodic theft opportunities to surface. Since theft is an everyday requirement to many addicts, they must be able to rely upon a ready and ongoing place in which to commit their acts. Thus, with the opening of retail stores each morning such offenders are also open for their own business of theft.

Shorthand Research

Based on the data presented above, a search was undertaken to learn the actual extent of overlap between shoplifting and drug addiction. The research method was simply to view court dockets of one major city court system, which had specialized courts for both retail theft and drug users. Dockets were searched over a ninety-day period for both courts. This short time span was chosen as multiple arrests within only three months would indicate an extremely active offender. The task was to see how many, if any, offenders had been booked into both retail theft court and drug court indicating an addiction issue was noted by authorities.

Findings

Retail Theft Court averaged 50 arrestees per day, or 250 a week, or 3,100 over the ninety-day period. Of that total 1,442 were booked into the court more than once over the time frame, indicating that at least this number of shoplifters might be considered professional offenders as opposed to the opportunistic amateur thief. Clearly, this percentage (47 percent) is drastically greater than the previously accepted figure of only 10 percent of shoplifters being professional offenders.

Over the same time frame Drug Court dealt with only 614 arrestees. Each such offender had been recognized as a probable addicted offender and was offered some sort of recovery related diversion from usual prosecution. The court dockets from Drug Court were scrutinized against those from Retail Theft Court. It was determined that 322 of the 614 total individuals appearing in Drug Court had also been booked into the Retail Theft Court over the same time period.

Conclusion

Findings disclose that more than one-half (52 percent) of all those brought before Drug Court over the time period in question were active shoplifters. This data would indicate that this form of theft is a preferred source of revenue gathering required to support their drug addiction.

An allied issue also surfaced in the course of this research in that it was also disclosed that a disproportionately large percentage of shoplifters entering Retail Theft Court were arrested at least twice over the ninety-day period. Thus, it would appear that the percentage of active professionals involved in shoplifting is far greater than previously recognized research indicated.

ARTICLE 35 — *A Conversation About Burglary*

Burglary is a crime which in some states is called breaking and entering. The elements of the offense deal with a forcible or unlawful entry into a dwelling, with the intent to commit a theft or other felony therein. A second classification is commercial burglary, which involves entry into a business. This generally occurs during hours when the store is not open to customers. The most common perception of burglary occurs when one knocks a door down, goes inside, and steals from the residence.

Note, however, that a theft is not always a required element of the offense. In some instances the forcible entry into a dwelling is actually followed by a sexual assault, or less frequently a physical attack. Quite often burglaries followed by a physical confrontation may be confused with the criminal offense of home invasion. The distinction between burglary and home invasion rests in the requirement that in a home invasion the offender must either know or reasonably expect that the dwelling broken into is occupied at the time of the entry.

The burglary versus home invasion issue becomes even more hazy when one considers that most burglaries leading up to sexual attack do not involve use of a forcible entry, but rather an illegal entry. There are two essential manners in which an illegal entry may be accomplished. The more common of the two illegal entries would involve the offender simply walking through the door of a dwelling left unlocked. A variation of that incident would occur by virtue of the offender climbing through an open window into the dwelling.

There is another type of illegal entry which occurs far less frequently, whereby an offender enters a place of business during normal hours of operation, then hides inside until the store closes, and then steals within.

Crime Classification

As noted, burglary is considered a property crime based on the usual motive for the act, which is monetary gain. However, lawmakers often have far greater concern over burglary offenses than most other property crimes in that the victims can find themselves in great jeopardy of serious attack in the course of burglary offenses.

Case Study

Major city police responded to a residential burglary alarm in an area nearby a large university campus. Upon arrival investigators found that the kitchen door had been forced open. The apartment had been ransacked, so a lookout message to other police units was sent to seek individuals carrying personal or household property in the area.

Once inside the police found an elderly woman semi-conscious in the dining room. She had countless burn marks up and down her arms, and had been forcibly raped.

Responding police units quickly located two suspects nearby carrying the proceeds of the crime.

It was quickly learned that the offenders had knocked on the kitchen door, heard no response from within, and so they went ahead and broke into the apartment. They were in the process of looting the place when the old lady, who was hard of hearing, awoke from a nap. She walked into the area where the offenders were gathering goods. The pair then decided to torture her with a lit cigarette, then took turns raping her.

While this case is extreme for its needless violence, it does serve to point out how vulnerable a victim one can quickly become when he/she surprises a burglar inside a dwelling. It is for this reason that although burglary is classified as a property crime, it is also regarded as a forcible felony for sentencing purposes.

Deadly Force Responses

Deadly force is a term concerned with police attempts at apprehending criminal suspects. Deadly force is generally defined as that force likely to cause death or great bodily harm. While there are just about as many laws on use of deadly force as there are states, the policies are often categorized in the following manner:

1) The FBI Standard for agents' use of deadly force is notable for its simplicity. Agents

may use deadly force when they reasonably believe that their life, or the life of another, is in immediate danger.

2) Many states allow that law enforcement officers may use deadly force in the apprehension of an armed offender.

3) It is also commonly stated that officers may use deadly force on a fleeing forcible felon.

Analysis

The FBI Standard states that when an agent is faced with shoot or be shot, he/she may shoot. Similarly, the FBI allows use of deadly force to prevent the probable death of victims of crimes, such as in a hostage situation.

When it is stated that officers may use deadly force in the apprehension of an armed offender, the key element thus is not the nature of the offender's initial crime, but rather the simple fact that he/she is armed while attempting to flee the police.

When lawmakers state that the police may use deadly force to apprehend a fleeing forcible felon, the concern is that if one has committed such a common forcible felony as murder, aggravated battery, sex offenses, or arson, that the risk is too great to allow the offender's escape. The thinking is that if one commits such an offense once, he/she is likely to do the same many times over if allowed to escape capture.

It is a commonly held belief that most forcible felons are likely to be armed at the time of the crime, and thus armed also at the time of their getaway attempt. However, the law does not state that the fleeing forcible felon must also be armed. Herein lies the issue surrounding the fact that burglary is a forcible felony offense.

Although burglaries do not typically result in violence, lawmakers are concerned due to the issues described in the case study. Though the initial intent of most burglaries is not to attack anyone, when surprised by victims, burglars will lash out violently. Thus the need to classify burglary as a forcible felony.

However, since burglary is so classified, the end result is that in many jurisdictions the police may legally shoot and kill an unarmed burglar attempting to make good his/her getaway. This condition is not well received among many observers.

nothing about the future can be proven to be incorrect. Readings of this nature pay the rent and are welcomed. As such, gypsies do not typically attempt larger frauds upon those customers.

By contrast, most potential victims are elderly females who visit gypsies for the purpose of making contact with deceased spouses. It is here that the gypsy manipulation of the vulnerable elderly occurs. During early visits the reader informs the victim that the dearly departed says hello and that they love and miss the victim. However, in-depth conversations with the deceased can only occur under more exacting conditions, which is extremely hard work, thus the cost is often thousands of dollars. Other times the elderly victims are told that they must divest themselves of excessive wealth in order to make the best possible contact with the loved one. Cons involving tens of thousands of dollars are common.

Based on their vulnerability the victims seldom confide in more lucid family members as to their actions. Even when the victim becomes aware of having been conned, they are not likely to contact the police due to embarrassment.

Distraction Thefts

Perhaps the most common gypsy con game involves a pair of offenders going to the door of an elderly resident. In one version of the con the victim is told by the gypsies that they are public utility workers assigned to check their water pressure. One offender will walk the victim to the basement so that he/she may run the water. Once the victim is safely away from the main floors of the home, the second offender will search for valuables without disturbing the appearance of the residence. Cash and jewelry are the most common items taken. By the time the valuables are missed, days and perhaps weeks have passed. Often the elderly victim never associates the gypsies' visit with the loss. Other times when the theft is understood, the victim may be too embarrassed to admit having been conned.

A second version of the homeowner con involves gypsies telling an elderly homeowner that their home does not meet city regulations in terms of roofing, gutters, or other housing items. The gypsies offer to do the repair at a very low price in order to see where the victim goes to get his/her cash. Once the money has been located, one offender will lead the victim to inspect the work to be done while the accomplice cleans out the cash source. They then say that they will return shortly with work supplies, then quickly vanish.

Major city police departments may have a fraud squad who specializes in con games. In smaller agencies, property crimes investigators work gypsy crimes. In either case gaining prosecutions against gypsies is ordinarily difficult. One major problem for

281

authorities is that a large percentage of victims are elderly and frail, and may suffer from dementia. When this occurs prosecution becomes nearly impossible without benefit of a lucid victim. Another difficulty lies in the fact that in distraction thefts there is no actual witness to the theft. The most the victim might be able to say is that a suspect must have been left alone in the home at the time of the crime. Such circumstantial evidence cases do not usually play well in criminal court. Lastly, there are certain cases where police investigators must rely upon a confession of the suspect in order to charge. What is certain is that gypsies will never make any type of incriminating statement to the authorities. To cooperate in any form with the police simply goes against the nature of the gypsy lifestyle.

INTRODUCTION TO PART IV

So who is right about crime causation and criminal behavior. After one hundred years of criminological theories, the theory continues as to the best possible answer as to why people commit crimes and what criminal behavior actually looks like.

Prior to the first edition of *Practical Criminology*, observers often rated theories of criminology based upon the extent to which research findings were able to be verified by theoretical statistics. By contrast the basis for this book was to review well-known theories and weigh their relative merits based upon the actual practical experiences of veteran street-wise working police.

In the five years since the first edition surfaced, a deeper comparative analysis of notable theories has been applied to what smart cops know about criminal behavior. More and more the greatest body of positive comparison falls to Walter B. Miller in his 1958 Lower-Class Culture analysis of criminal behavior.

Miller points to crime as being a normal reflection of lower-class cultural norms. Within this context lower-class street corner groups seek status and recognition by routinely acting out crimes in a manner which seems normal within such lower-class communities. Albert Cohen describes this condition as lower-class society "turns middle class values and norms upside down" which smoothly leads to the carrying out of crimes.

It is also important to recognize the work of Edwin Sutherland (1883-1950) for having developed the theory of Differential Association, which essentially states that criminal behavior is learned. Certainly any bright observer aware of the extent to which our prisons serve a "college of crime" would agree with this learning theory.

The first portion of Part IV deals extensively with the work of Miller — with the presentation of numerous examples of the many ways in which his theory is readily acted out on the mean streets of lower-class society. The second segment contains a brief summary of prime examples of Sutherland's consideration of the exacting ways in which criminal behavior is a learned behavior.

PART IV

WALTER B. MILLER

Lower-Class Society Theory

Overview

That crime is normal in many lower-class communities is certainly a prevailing theme of this book. What that statement means is that crime and criminal behavior is every bit as much a part of such societies as are schools, churches, and after-school care facilities. In such communities both the criminal element and law abiding individuals routinely know what crimes take place and who committed them.

It is therefore little wonder what Walter B. Miller wrote in 1958. His work on lower-class culture portrayed delinquent behavior as a normal reflection of lower-class cultural norms, which is produced through three processes.

1) Heeding the essential expectations of lower-class culture often automatically involves law violations.
2) If there are options available, the non-law abiding choice frequently will provide a better and faster return for less investment.
3) There are certain recurring situations that simply demand the commission of illegal acts.

Members of lower-class street corner groups are motivated to achieve status through a distinctive tradition which is contrary to commonly accepted middle-class values. While such status is indeed based on having become recognized for the commission of deviant acts, that matters little by virtue of the fact that within such subcultures deviance is not really seen as negative force.

Six focal concerns characterize lower-class culture according to Miller, which are defined as areas or issues that occupy a great amount of time and consideration on the part of lower-class individuals. They are trouble, toughness, smartness, excitement, fate, and autonomy.

Miller's perspective of lower-class cultures does fall in line extremely closely with modern urban crime-fighting experiences of lower-class crime, and forms the best possible practical application of a single theory of criminology.

Trouble

Miller discusses "trouble" as a focal point of lower-class youth's concern. In a setting where breaking laws is often expedient, it requires such actors to come to expect that trouble will at least occasionally come their way in the form of police interest in their activities. To the extent that many criminal acts are premeditated, offenders realize and appreciate that a certain percentage of the time they will become subjects of the criminal justice system.

However, upon closer observation of lower-class life, many criminal offenders take the position that nearly every aspect of the police investigation must go the law's way for them to be arrested and charged. Later, those charged must also lose their case in court. In a nutshell, lower-class offenders frequently victimize persons they know in the belief that urban victims infrequently file police reports. When a report is made, the particular police investigator must have both time and interest in their investigation. Later, when arrested, many suspects feel confident in their "smartness" to the extent that they will somehow be capable of convincing the police of their innocence. Finally, when charged, their chances of being found not guilty are often good. Thus the issue of being investigated is not the same element of trouble as eventually being convicted.

There is also a question of whether or not being convicted of a crime and sentenced to jail or prison time actually constitutes "trouble" as it is usually seen. Consider the following general features of lower-class society.

1) A prison sentence in lower-class places is seen as being a normal fact of life.
2) Actually serving a prison sentence is not typically a cause of fear as most of the inmates are either friends or associates of the new inmate from the lower-class society.

3) Prison inmates are ranked according to the amount of daring of their crimes and by their ability to control inmate life by their relative violence level. Thus prison life is often a cause for increased criminal status.
4) Prisons are by far the best place for less experienced criminals to learn specifics as to the best and most successful criminal tactics and techniques from more experienced inmates.

Summary

While most members of lower-class society are likely to agree that remaining free on the "outside" is by far preferable over incarceration, the trouble factor others might attach to serving a prison sentence is not the same to the lower-class offender. Other forms of "trouble" such as street gang rivalries and drug rip-offs are seen as being a normal byproduct of the society in which they live and function. Within this context "trouble" is generally accepted as being manageable.

Lower-Class Awareness of Toughness

Status within the criminal subculture is an important feature of the lower-class culture. In other socio-economic settings people win praise and admiration for academic, athletic, and artistic prowess. In the inner-city, members of the community who carry out the most daring criminal acts often take on legendary status due to their extreme fearlessness or "heart."

In other portions of this book the issue that "crime is normal" in lower-class communities is addressed. There is so much violence in such areas that members of the criminal community and honest people alike come in ongoing contact with massive amounts of bloodshed. Seeing both the actual acts of violence taking place, as well as victims of violence, leads to a numbing of sensitivity to crime.

Children lose their innocence quickly in such lower-class areas. Pre-school age kids are routinely able to identify makes and models of firearms the way other children know "Kermit the Frog." And little children along with all other residents do know the identity of the robbers, home invaders, and killers.

Community awareness of toughness and fearlessness is common knowledge in lower-class areas. Criminal offenders do wish to build their tough reputations and must therefore admit to their criminal deeds so that they can get what they see as their due recognition for their acts. Such admissions occur with little, if any, fear that members of the lower-class community will inform on them to the police. This is primarily due to the belief that criminals themselves will not talk and that the honest majority of residents do not wish to get involved in the criminal business of others. To a great extent the criminals are correct on both counts. Criminals hate the police and stick together, and honest people fear the criminals and often mistrust the police.

The openness and acceptance of crime and violence in lower-class societies may be best illustrated by the association of trophy keeping to memorialize criminal exploits. It is not unusual for home invaders to take a photo of the proceeds of the crime, along with their weapons and ski masks, and other tools of the act. Such photos are a celebration of a successfully carried out crime for children and visitors to see.

The extent to which tough criminals are convinced that their work may be safely publicized is perhaps best illustrated by the great volume of crime information postings on Facebook and other social media sites. Such brashness on the part of criminals illustrates both the extent of their self-promotion, as well as their belief that such self-promotion will remain a secret among thousands.

The Value of Toughness as Practiced on the Streets

Over one-half a century ago Walter Miller (1955) noted that within the lower-class culture the quality of toughness was valued. The behaviors of urban street gang members and other inner-city residents have proven the spot-on merit of Miller's early observations.

It is to be noted that urban society has a tongue of its own. And much of what it has to say greatly honors toughness. Within this culture there is no greater compliment than to say that someone "has a lot of heart." Within this context the word "heart" means fearlessness and fearlessness means courage. While the rest of the population also measures courage, the relative actions are often toward opposite ends and goals.

Firefighters and soldiers are among many portions of the workforce who safeguard human lives at the risk of their own personal safety. At the same time "heart" plays a nearly identical role within the lower-class community, because the commission of crimes can be exceedingly dangerous business. Just as certain fearful police officers are able to reduce personal risk, so do certain criminals as well. The police officer may reduce his/her relative dangers by choosing to work in low crime-rate areas and by moving slowly to dangerous calls for service in the hope that the armed offender will be long gone before his/her arrival.

In a similar manner, the inner-city criminal lacking toughness or "heart" may reduce his/her potential danger by taking on less dangerous tasks such as retail theft as opposed to armed robbery. So it is easy to understand that the truly tough members of lower-class society are honored for their "heart."

The more daring the crime the greater the danger, not only to crime victims but to the offenders as well. The armed robber must consider that when approaching a potential victim on the street, he/she may actually be confronting another person armed with a gun.

Off-duty police officers carry firearms as do many private citizens in the interest of self-protection. So what might have been intended to be a nice, clean, armed robbery might well turn into a shootout with the would-be robber's death. Similarly, the armed robber may be intercepted in the act by working police with the same result. Therefore, the more daring the criminal act, the higher accord from lower-class society.

Case Study

In one major urban city four men were all paroled from prison within weeks of one another for unrelated murder convictions. Each had grown up in the same housing project and was within a year of one another in age. And each had taken on the status of urban legend for his willingness to kill, either due to what was seen as justifiable rage and retaliation, or for significant monetary gain.

Each individual had proven his toughness and "heart" to the extent that members of the community frequently told stories about their criminal exploits. The four of them were all given welcome home parties by friends and families upon their return from prison. It was at one such gathering that the quartet decided to pool the strength of their infamous reputations in a most profitable manner.

It is common knowledge that illegal street drugs afford the greatest amount of profit from urban crime, and so their plan was hatched. Virtually all the street drug retailers stock up on Thursdays for the long weekend ahead. Due to the wide-open nature of such drug operations, it was common knowledge where the dealers lived and dealt from.

So on the following Thursday evening the four recent parolees loaded their newly acquired firearms and moved from one drug house to the next, robbing each of large quantities of drugs as well as cash and weapons. In each such armed robbery the victim-dealers had a choice to make: They could take on these urban legends renowned for their eagerness to carry out extreme violence and shoot it out with them, or they could turn over their valuables.

In each case for a month's time the dealers surrendered to the quartet's tough reputation and handed over tens of thousands of dollars at a time. Nobody was willing to shoot it out with the infamous offenders.

Finally, the group of victimized drug dealers had a summit meeting where it was decided that something had to be done. Though there were more than a dozen dealers present, none were willing to go to war against the collective "heart" of the rip-off quartet. However, a plan was formulated. One dealer named Farquar Feliz had been robbed on three consecutive Thursdays and had lost more than $30,000.00 in drugs and cash. It was decided that he would do the unheard of and contact the police and report the crimes.

Clearly both the police and prosecutors were stunned that a heroin dealer had actually made police reports of having been robbed of heroin, but their victim stated he would gladly go to court and tell what happened. The first three offenders were arrested without incident. They were so surprised that a dealer had reported the rip-offs that they were not prepared to take action against the police. However, by the time it came to arrest the fourth member, he had been alerted as to what was taking place. So when the police knocked on his door, he jumped out of a bedroom window and landed on cement eight stories below. Proving his toughness one more time, he was able to drag a fractured leg behind him for several blocks before being arrested.

All four of the urban rip-offs were convicted and went back to prison for long terms. However not before they had parlayed their infamous reputations into huge monetary gain. Miller himself would have agreed at the extent to which they had proven his theory as to the value of urban toughness.

The Evolution of Toughness

In the 1950s when Miller's work first surfaced, toughness was acted out primarily with fists. A decade later lower-class street gangs became armed with firearms (see Article 21 on Black P Stone Nation). After several years of shooting and killing rival gang members, street gang leaders realized that they had boundless toughness under their control — sometimes several thousand gang members. They came to realize that there was no money in shooting gang rivals.

As described in the Stone article, they were among the first street gangs to become financially comfortable by using their collective "heart" to extort and intimidate members of the community. Their leader, Jeff Fort, was bright and realized that he had over six thousand members of his organization who were all waiting their respective opportunities to prove their "heart" and toughness by shooting and killing persons upon request. Fort also realized that there was no money in killing Black Disciple gang rivals, but there was a fortune to be made in extorting from school children, merchants, and eventually criminals in the community.

Final Thoughts on Toughness

Walter Miller speaks to the issue that a disproportionately large percentage of lower-class tough kids come from fatherless homes. Much of Miller's work focuses on boys' needs to escape their female-dominated homes and therefore search for their own male images on the streets.

Another aspect of this condition stems from the fact that very young, single mothers may lack the parenting tools and maternal instincts to care for their children adequately. In many public housing settings it is easy to see countless sets of "stair-step" kids, with ten-year-olds given the task of caring for seven-year siblings, and on down to where five-year-olds are supposed to be looking after toddlers. The result of such situations is often that such children lack both nurturing and praise which kids in other settings routinely get.

Placed in such a sink-or-swim setting, many lower-class children are susceptible to various forms of neglect and abuse, which leads to extreme confusion as the children must attempt to figure out questions for themselves, which otherwise would have been explained to them by attentive parents. It makes perfect sense that many such children become frustrated and also angry at being so alone, and clearly anger leads to acting out poorly. Once identified as a child who gets in trouble, defiance results and toughness safeguards the child from harm's way.

Smartness

Walter Miller identified the fact that lower-class youths prided themselves for their smartness. Within this context it is important to qualify this term by which "smartness" and "use of intelligence" to traditional means are not at all the same. To the urban youth "smartness" is taken to mean "to outsmart" others. This definition includes outsmarting the police who may ask questions and accuse smart youths about their possible involvement in criminal activity. To outsmart also applies to members of the community who may be victimized by the smart youth. Such smartness might range from the simple, such as selling what to the buyer is a sealed box containing a new television set, only to get home and find that what he/she actually bought was a box of rocks, to extremely complicated schemes designed to defraud the public.

Feigning Respectability

Most field interrogations involve the police stopping and questioning criminal suspects whom they have not previously encountered. Police have the right to question individuals when they reasonably believe that the suspect is committing, has committed, or is about to commit a crime. Such questioning of strangers often begins with a police attempt to determine the suspect's identity and his/her criminal history. Once the inquiring officer verifies that the suspect does have a criminal past, the police become convinced that their inquiries do have merit to the extent that the person being questioned does have an arrest record.

The "smart" criminal is aware of this basic police task, and therefore understands the prime importance of convincing the police that he is a respectable fellow and not a part of the criminal community. Smart criminals know that their ability to convince the police that they are respectable citizens often brings a quick end to the field interrogation process. When the officer has been outsmarted by the criminal suspect, the officer often ends the interaction by saying, "Sorry to bother you." It is then that the smart criminal walks away laughing on the inside at having put one over on the less smart police officer.

In many other situations experienced street cops know who everyone on the street is, thus it becomes impossible for smart criminals to take on the roll of respectability. However, in such cases, smart criminals can use their cunning to convince the inquiring police that this time they are not guilty of criminal wrongdoing as suspected.

The ability to outsmart people is highly thought of in lower-class communities and specifically within the criminal subculture. The term used to best describe this practice is to "shoot angles" in order to profit from such interactions.

Case Study

Upon arriving in prison one of the first questions new inmates ask is for detailed information about institutional social workers and other mental health counselors. Such counselors have significant input into the institutional view of inmates. The highly cooperative inmate gets favors based upon positive mental health reports from counselors.

Smart inmates quickly learn what drives a certain mental health counselor. Certain such individuals are experts and most concerned with physical or sexual child abuse. Others may be centered on the effects upon inmates of having been raised in a single-family home, or by the sudden death of persons close to the patient. And so within a matter of hours of having arrived in prison, the new inmate knows each counselor's sensitive points; and then quickly parlays whatever the given issue may be to his/her advantage in terms of garnering the sympathy of his/her counselor. Before one knows it, every inmate on a caseload has been the victim of whatever issue makes the counselor tick.

Within this context it is important to note that Miller's use of the term "smartness" is not a matter of relative intelligence as measured by IQ testing. Certainly many prison counselors are far more bright than the average inmate. However the key issue as to the lower-class use of "smartness" is that such persons are in no way bound by the truth in the application of their smartness. Similarly, the prison social worker or others being "played" by the criminal wrongly expects the truth, and naively accepts manipulative lies as being valid. Simply put, the "smart" lower-class criminal uses lies as weapons as he/she seeks to gain whatever financial or emotional edge he/she seeks as being the outcome of his/her plan to "outsmart" others.

Thus the inmate who falsely claims to having been tortured by fire by his mother's addicted boyfriend is likely to gain certain institutional favors suggested by the naïve prison counselor.

Excitement

Rogers and Mays interpret Walter Miller's findings that lower-class youths seek excitement in their work, *Juvenile Delinquency and Juvenile Justice*. Their primary example centers around a discussion whereby young people go "bar-hopping" to avoid boredom. They point out that drinking around young women and talking to the women of other men may be risky business. While that analysis may be accurate, it is not the type of excitement that many tough and smart, young lower-class residents seek most often.

To the street-smart member of lower-class society a night drinking on the town may indirectly create moments of excitement, but in reality for actual members of the criminal subculture excitement is clearly of their own making.

A significantly large percentage of highly paid professional athletes are from lower-class upbringings. Therefore many of the behaviors they learned and valued as youths remain as desirable actions as wealthy young adults. So it is not surprising that groups of football and basketball players carry a high and often menacing profile as they visit bars and nightclubs. The fact that most professional athletes are among the most physically strong members of society adds to their ability to court excitement and often acting out actual toughness.

However, Walter Miller's observations of lower-class individuals seeking excitement does move far beyond simply visiting bars and night clubs. Earlier on in the analysis of Miller's work much was said about lower-class residents gaining legendary status by their extreme toughness and "heart." It is this very set of tough and fearless actions which do create an atmosphere of excitement. Simply put, violent behaviors do create excitement.

Determining Criminal Status

Article 12, Street Policing Status in this work, discusses the issue that not all police officers are regarded in the same ways. A disproportionately small percentage of police officers are responsible for a very large percentage of all arrests for violence.

Major violent crime arrests are made largely by officers who race to "hot calls" for service, such as robberies in progress and shots fired on the street. Many other violent crimes are solved by officers who engage in many field interrogations on the public way. If any given officer stops and questions thirty or forty suspicious persons in the course of a tour of duty, it is likely that such inquiries will lead to a certain number of arrests.

What seems to separate such highly active police officers from other mainstream members of the force is that the most active officers are notable for their fearlessness. Less active and more fearful officers who wish to avoid direct contact with potentially dangerous suspects simply do not stop suspicious persons on the street, and they do not race to hot calls. By laying back and allowing other officers to be the first to arrive at a crime scene, they also limit the risks attached to having to confront the armed and dangerous offender.

Exactly the same premise is true of members of the criminal subculture. Offenders who cannot cope with taking dangerous risks simply commit less dangerous crimes, where they are not called upon to exert violence, and also where the police are even more likely not to use deadly force in their arrest. Armed robbers are excellent candidates for being shot by the police; shoplifters are not.

Therefore, it is the most actively violent members of lower-class society who take the greatest risks; first the risk of having to shoot and kill their victim or someone else, and secondly the probability is great that they might end up in a gun battle with the police in the course of attempting to make good their getaway.

A major premise of this work is that the most active police officers and the most active members of the criminal subculture, which Walter Miller studied, are much like one another in that both are great risk takers and often actually delight at the violence and excitement of their similar work toward opposite ends.

Fear works effectively with most people in the sense that individuals are likely to practice a certain amount of caution when placed in potentially dangerous situations.

This type of buffer works to save a certain number of injuries and death, not only to both the police and criminals, but among the general population as well. That said, it remains a mistake to assume that all persons placed in potentially dangerous situations do respond with fear anxiety.

For many individuals danger does lead to excitement and an adrenalin flow which is actually one form of a natural high. Just as the most active street cops create their own excitement by the manner in which they go about their work, many members of the criminal community create their own form of excitement by their criminal deeds.

It is important to grasp the concept that in all types of violent crimes the offender is stating, "Do as I say or you face great harm," either by words to that effect or by their actions. Being a prostitute is a dangerous job, so they need the protection of a pimp. While the prostitute stands on a street corner luring her dates, her pimp stands conspicuously nearby sending the clear-cut message that to hurt his lady is to bring about great violence and its corresponding excitement. So it should not be a surprise that members of the criminal community engage in job selection based essentially by their willingness to act violently and the subsequent excitement.

Fate

To many the issue of fate is closely connected with the issue of luck. Gamblers often believe in fate — that this time they have certainly conjured up the winning roulette or lottery number. Within such contexts individuals see themselves as being able to collect large amounts of assets with little, if any investment. In that sense it may be seen as something of a shallow perspective of limited value and requiring little, if any faith.

By contrast, fate is often a matter of life and death to many members of dangerous work. Within this context both violent criminals and street police are involved in job functions which at any time might cause serious injury or death. Members of lower-class culture who routinely are involved in violent, risky, and dangerous acts are often asked the question by others as to whether or not they are most certainly afraid to be constantly placed in such danger. Ironically, the police who respond and investigate such crimes are also asked whether or not they too are afraid of confronting the most dangerous members of society.

In both situations what is really being asked is whether or not the person is afraid to die. The most active street criminals as well as the most active police officers both plunge head first into potentially dangerous confrontations with the other. Such behaviors in confronting great violent dangers can only be accomplished without fears that would otherwise moderate or temper their actions. Violent offenders shoot up a busy urban street and then flee down a dark alley toward freedom. The most fearless street cops race on foot into the darkness of the alley with the knowledge that the offender might whirl and shoot at them at any second.

In such situations neither the gunman nor the officer is restrained by his/her own fear anxiety. And the reason for this is most likely that they look at both their work and life from a fatalistic perspective. Courting ongoing dangers to this degree is best accomplished by individuals who take the simple attitude that "when their time comes, they're going (to die) and there's nothing that can be done about it."

Fate as Superstition

Many criminals are much like athletes in the sense that they tend to continue the use of whatever techniques or methods of operation have worked successfully in the past. A hitter may wear the same socks he wore while hitting a game-winning home run in the previous game. Similarly, a criminal offender may rob the same store a second or third time just as long as he keeps successfully getting away with the crimes.

Such reliance upon fate by way of method of operation is a common occurrence. Bright police investigators search regularly for apparent patterns of crime by comparing similar criminal offenses in order to determine the likelihood that one person or group of people may be responsible for multiple offenses. Investigators typically compare physical descriptions of suspects, dates, times, and locations of the criminal offenses, as well as the precise method of operation carried out by the offenders. In this manner police investigators develop a good idea as to whether or not the multiple offenses are the work of the same person or people. Similarly, investigators are also able to make educated predictions as to when and where the next such offense may occur.

Despite the police intelligence gathering described above, many criminals will continue to follow exactly the same method of operation based upon their connection and concern for the role of fate they consider to be valid.

In one such notable case, a gifted basketball player from a major urban city became addicted to heroin and needed a way to support his drug habit. For three days in a row during early afternoon hours he entered the same corner grocery store wearing a ski mask and brandishing a shotgun. Each time he fled with various amounts of cash. Of course, the success the criminal suspect realized was essentially due to the fact that the police simply never considered that anyone would press his luck in the way he had by carrying out a trio of robberies on three consecutive days.

On the fourth day police tactical officers hid behind the grocery counter and were not disappointed when the armed gunman arrived and announced yet another robbery. The police apprehended him without incident, then asked him why he continued robbing the same store. He seemed astonished by the police question, stating that he had every intention of continuing his successful crime pattern until he was caught. "Why quit what works?" he said.

Autonomy

Miller states that autonomy is seen as being a valuable part of lower-class society. This is not surprising in view of a variety of social conditions in such communities. It is important to recognize that when one speaks in terms of crime being normal within a subculture, we are actually looking at many forms of criminal actors.

For example, both male and female members of lower-class society have dual roles, at once committing criminal acts and creating children. Both male and female drug addicts become parents. While their respective intentions may be great in terms of being active and effective parents, the reality is usually that the need to get and use their next drug supercedes all of those good intentions. People rob, break in, steal, and sell their bodies to feed their addictions. That does not leave a lot of time for attending pre-school parents' meetings, or for reading to their kids.

Addiction and the preoccupation of gaining the required finances for drugs creates major forms of social disorganization. Active parents are able to wake up in the morning so that they can also wake their kids up for school. Easy for the organized parent, all but impossible for the addicted parent. So the result is all too often that kids from such backgrounds do not often get to school, so they suffer the consequences by not learning as they should. Not being able to perform well in the school setting leads to truancy as the child wishes to avoid the discomfort and embarrassment of poor class performance.

Once the cycle of missing school sets in, many lower-class children are left with learning of another sort on the streets on their own. Thus one might argue that for many lower-class children their eventual search for autonomy is actually something of a secondary response to their inability to find stability in the usual places. Social problems surrounding their parents such as single-family households, teenage pregnancy, criminal interests, and drug addiction all act against the child's ability to gain any sort of comfort within the school. Thus the school experience is traded for another form of learning which aids the process of autonomy.

Edwin Sutherland

One of the earliest and strongest theories of criminology stemmed from the works of Edwin Sutherland (1883-1950).

Edwin Sutherland received his Ph.D. degree from the University of Chicago in 1913 but he established his reputation as a long-time faculty member at Indiana University. Among his students was Donald R. Cressey, who later became a colleague. Today a distinguished criminologist in his own right, Cressey has helped preserve the Sutherland heritage through their textbook, *Criminology,* which is now in its tenth edition.

Although Sellin and Sutherland influenced each other, Sutherland developed his own theory drawing on other strands of scholarship. For example, he was greatly influenced by the work of Gabriel Tarde (1843-1904), an early advocate of learning theory relative to criminality. According to Tarde's famous laws of imitation, first, human beings imitate the fashions and customs of others; the greater is the interaction among people, the greater will be the imitation of others. Second, persons of inferior status often imitate those of superior status. And third, if two mutually exclusive fashions or customs conflict, the newer one will be more widely imitated. Sutherland also held that at the core of moral responsibility are personal identity or self-concept plus such basic ingredients as customs, interests, and education.

Sutherland's doctrine of how crime occurs, or differential association, is fundamentally a form of learning theory and consists of nine interlocking phases. It has been termed a developmental explanation of criminal behavior.

1) *Criminal behavior is learned.* This is not only an emphasis on learning in its own right but also a rejection of biological explanations. Sutherland believed that Lombroso had set back the cause of criminology for perhaps half a century.

2) *Such learning occurs through social interaction with other persons.* This interaction includes not only verbal communication but also cues or gestures, which also convey meaning.

3) *Criminal behavior is learned principally in intimate personal groups.* This suggests that the roots of crime and delinquency are most apt to be discovered in the socialization experiences of a person's primary groups (e.g., family, peer, work). This principle also minimizes the role of the mass media — the impersonal agencies of communication — in the learning of criminal behavior.

4) *This learning process includes not only the techniques of committing crimes but also the molding of personal attitudes, motives, drives, and rationalizations for deviant behavior.* Antisocial behavior is cultivated through a favorable environment offering such things as emotional support, a sustaining rationale, and collective approval. In the case of professional criminals, this would include complex techniques beyond the ordinary access of amateur offenders.

5) *The specific direction of drives and motives is learned from definitions of the legal codes as unfavorable or favorable.* This proposition is akin to Sellin's emphasis on cultural norms or conduct norms. In a complex society such as the United States, these definitions are almost always mixed

with the consequences of culture conflict in relation to the legal codes. In some instances, the person may be so sheltered, or surrounded by others of a given ideology, that he or she falls on one side or the other.

6) *A person becomes delinquent because of an excess of such definitions favorable to law violators, compared with those definitions unfavorable to them.* This, asserted Sutherland, is the principle of differential association. It refers to both criminal and anti-criminal influences and combines counteracting forces. The crux of criminality or delinquency is in one's communal and personal relationships, through which the surrounding culture is assimilated. When individuals break the law, they do so because of contacts with antisocial patterns, together with isolation from law-abiding patterns.

7) *Differential associations may vary in terms of four modalities: frequency, duration, priority, and intensity.* The first pair seems self-evident. Priority refers to the sequential element of associations. For example, this modality assumes the importance of exposures and social interaction during early childhood. Delinquent behavior developed early may persist throughout one's life. Intensity pertains to emotion and status, including qualities such as loyalty, esteem, love, commitment,

honor, and fear. Gang delinquency or organized crime are examples.

8) *The criminal learning process employs all of the mechanisms that are employed in any other learning.* Here Sutherland wanted to distance himself from Tarde's more superficial notion of imitation. Sutherland believed learning to be far more complex, involving conscious and unconscious elements encompassing virtually every phase of human adaptation.

9) *Although criminal behavior is an expression of general needs and values, it is not explained by them, because noncriminal behavior is an expression of the same needs and values.* Here Sutherland pointed out that thieves generally steal in order to obtain money, but likewise, honest laborers work in order to gain money. In short, he stressed that people do not become offenders simply because they want money, are unhappy, or are seeking status, because these all are valid motives for law-abiding behavior. Instead, criminal behavior represents a unique, deviant response to legitimate drives for prestige, happiness, success, wealth, or any other worthy goal. Although learning may stem from similar motives for all human beings, each person learns to express them in ways compatible with such ties as ethnic group, social class, and loved ones.

When youths are left to themselves at a younger age than usual, they are susceptible to coming in contact with an excess of interactions with members of the criminal community. This great number of opportunities to be influenced by those who do conduct criminal activity results in two conditions: first the child accepts the criminal acts of others as being valid, and secondly the child learns the specific ways to carry out such acts. Just as youths from other settings learn important lessons in athletics, dance, or academics, the lower-class youth learns such lessons as where to steal, how to fire guns, or where to run after having robbed someone.

Such lessons in what is seen as deviance in other socio-economic settings act to instill the criminal knowledge required to actually become autonomous at very young ages, often even before their teen years. Within this context autonomy for the lower-class youth means that

1) They have the street corner society as a place of comfort.
2) They have a means to a regular income despite their failure in the school setting.
3) They are able to grow a positive reputation for their criminal prowess.

In summary, the lower-class youth replaces their negative school and home experiences with the lower-class street corner society which allows them total freedom of movement absent from all forms of adult direction. Such comfort is typically supported by the companionship of other youths on the same path, and with this comes a sense of freedom and autonomy.

Many junior-high-school-age kids in the inner city earn as much as several hundred dollars a day by riding their expensive BMX bikes around the perimeter of a street-corner drug operation. Their job is simply to whistle to signal the approach of police cars. It is important to note that a ten-year-old kid can create what they see as a ton of fun for themselves with an income of more than $1,000.00 per week.

As Miller pointed out, lower-class society recognizes and appreciates criminal status in the way that the middle-class responds favorably to kids winning dance and athletic competitions. Such criminal reputations are recognized and grow each time the lower-class child outsmarts the police or commits a daring criminal act. Do note that anyone making $1,000.00 per week has the financial means to open their own drug operation which often leads to the autonomy which comes from illegally making what amounts to literally unlimited amounts of money. Today's ten-year-old on his bike warning that the police are nearby is tomorrow's millionaire as a teenager.

Great wealth buys autonomy.

In Closing

A book on criminology seemingly would be incomplete without the author offering his own theory as to why individuals commit criminal offenses . . .

Violent behavior breeds violence. Children may be subjected to issues of violent behavior in one of two primary ways: They may fall victim to violence in their own home, and they may also see it all around them within their community.

Where a small child is concerned, loud, harsh talk may be taken as one level of violent behavior. In more severe cases they may be victims of spanking, slaps, or worse. In certain cultures statements such as "I'm gonna' whip you, boy," have survived generations of threats and actual practice, and remains an acceptable method of parenting. Whippings may be accomplished with such household items as hairbrushes and belts; and when taken to a child, the act is extreme physical violence.

Adults who lack impulse control and therefore scream, swear, and punish their children by inflicting physical harm become the child's role model. Modeling of violence may also extend to the common nature of violent street crime, which is often all around children in many communities. The notion that "crime is normal" is everywhere around inner-city children.

When children see violence as a common response to conflict, the result is nearly inevitable that the influenced child will see that as an acceptable mode of behavior. Thus, when confronted by potential or actual conflict, they are likely to act out just as those role models near them.

Lastly, in many communities violent behavior results in high status for the actor. As such the child learning to use violence due to the above causes may also see status-related acclaim for violent actions, therefore reinforcing that type of behavior. When such violence is acted out, the child also learns that acts such as robbery, which call for either the threat of force or its actual use, may also profit financially for acting as they have learned to act.